The Holy Land I Love

Classic Scenes from Ancient Bible Sites

Lithographs by
DAVID ROBERTS

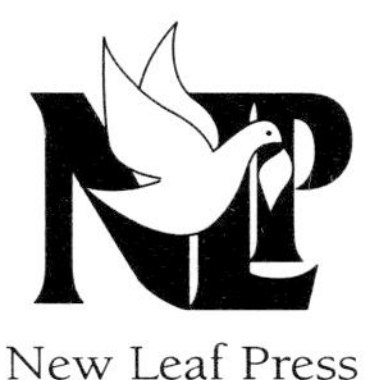

New Leaf Press

CONTENTS:

Accompanying each painting are abridged excerpts from the diary of **David Roberts (in bold text)**, and historical descriptions written by Rev. George Croly, who lived at the time of the artist in the mid 19th century.

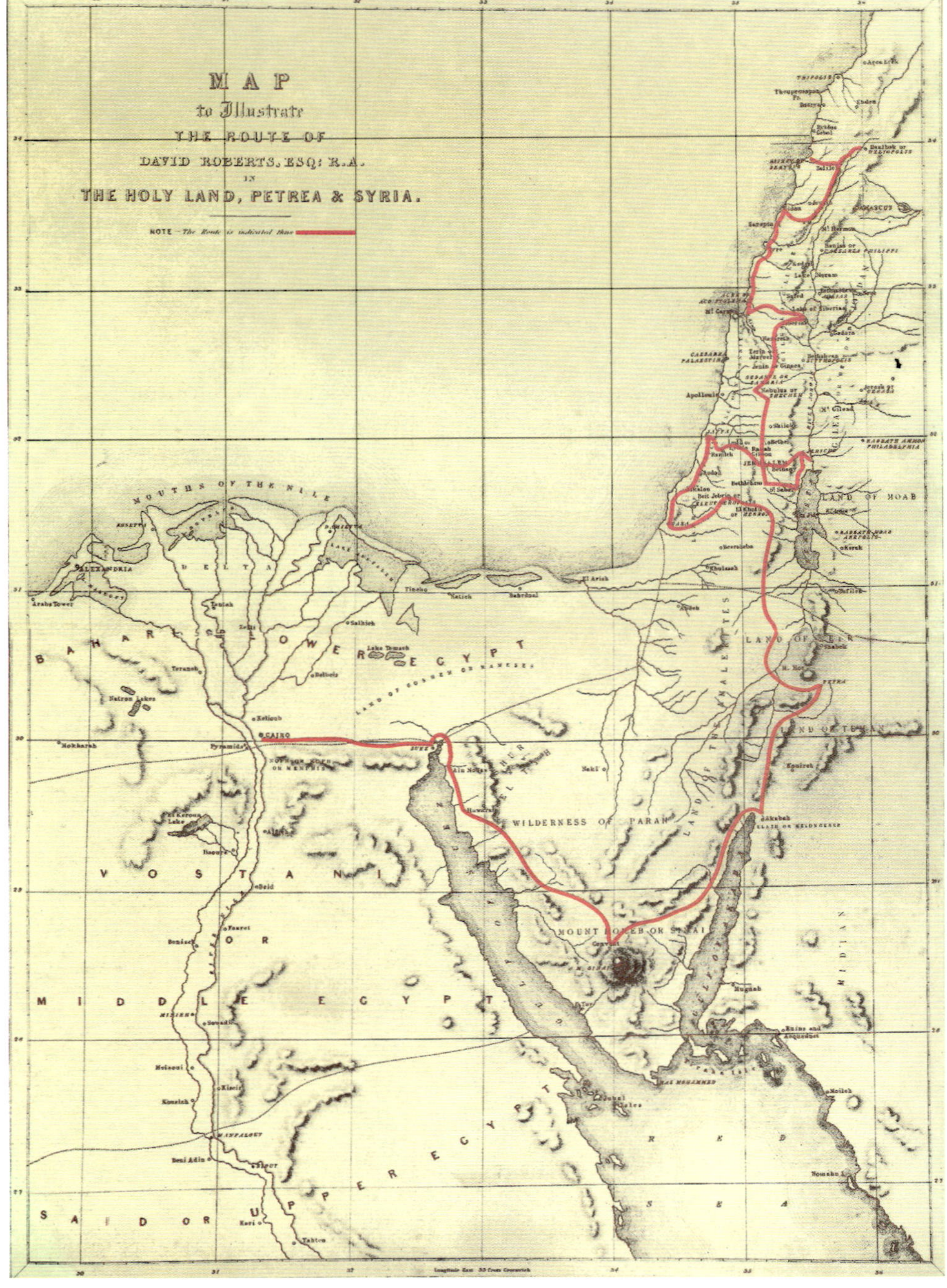

Text and lithographs courtesy of the Victoria & Albert Museums Library, London.

ISBN: 0-89221-517-8

Cover Design: Janell Robertson

All Scripture quotations are from the King James Version of the Bible.

Printed in Israel.

David Roberts was born at Stockbridge, near Edinburgh, October 24th, 1796: his early love of art may in some measure be traced to his mother, to whom he was devotedly attached. She was a native of the ancient episcopal town of St. Andrews and often spoke to him of the magnificent remains of the cathedral and monastic edifices of this once-celebrated seat of learning. These conversations influenced his taste for art towards that particular department which he may be said to have made his own, for there was scarcely an old castle or ruined chapel in or around his native town that he did not visit and sketch when a boy. By the advice of Graham, director of the "Trustees Academy" at Edinburgh, and the master of Wilkie and Allan, young Roberts, at the early age of ten years, was apprenticed to a house-painter named Gavin Beugo, who probably gave the lad some little instruction in drawing; beyond this, we believe, he has never been indebted to a single individual.

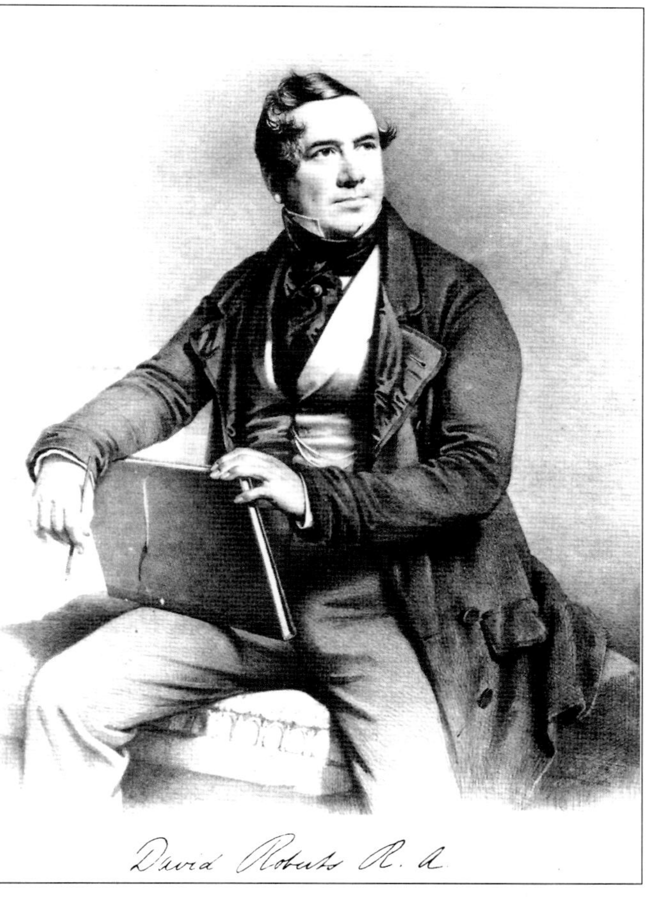

Having served a long and wearisome apprenticeship of seven years to Beugo, a harsh and over-bearing master, we hear of him in 1818, as assistant scenepainter at the Pantheon. In the following year, he became principal painter at the Theatre Royal, Glasgow, and in 1820 and 1821, at the Theatre Royal, Edinburgh. Before the latter year expired, his fame had reached the ears of the then lessee of Drury Lane, the celebrated Elliston, who offered him an engagement for three years.

From this point of time, the history of Roberts as a painter in oil really commences, his first picture being exhibited at the British institution in 1824. The first picture exhibited at the Academy by Roberts was "View of Rouen Cathedral," in 1826. Notwithstanding the incessant demands upon his time during the early period of his career, he found frequent opportunities for visiting the continent, for many of his exhibited pictures were subjects sketched in France, Germany, and Belgium, while his own native land was not forgotten: every successive year during the lifetime of his parents, did he visit them. On these occasions he was accustomed to make excursions through various parts of Scotland containing remarkable ancient edifices, of which he made drawings.

Roberts was elected associate to the Academy in the year 1838, but before the election of Roberts as a junior member of the Academy, he was making preparations for the most important event of his life, namely, a journey to Palestine, Egypt, and Syria; this was an undertaking he had long contemplated, and it seems to have been entered upon solely from a love of artistic adventure. Supplied with a letter of introduction from the Foreign Office to Colonel Campbell, Consul-General for Egypt, Roberts started from England on his great and hazardous expedition in August, 1838, taking the route by Paris and Marseilles. He arrived in Egypt by the end of September, 1838. In February, 1839, Roberts left Cairo to cross the desert by way of Suez, Mount Sinai and Petra. Having visited the most remarkable places from "Dan to Beer-sheba," illustrative with biblical history, he returned to England in the latter part of 1839 after an absence of about eleven months.

The fruits of this expedition are too well known to require pointing out that "Roberts' Holy Land" has a world-wide reputation; nothing of a similar character has ever been produced that can bear comparsion with it. Roberts, after one year of his return from his journey to the Holy Land, was elected full member of the Royal Academy. He was awarded with honors, especially at the International Exhibition held in Paris in the year 1855. He died at the age of 68, on 25 November 1864, and is buried in Norwood Cemetery. (from *The Art Journal*, 1858)

INTRODUCTION

To visit the Holy Land, and make drawings of the scene of sacred history and the antiquities of Egypt, had been, long before this journey was undertaken by Mr. Roberts, the brightest of his anticipation as an artist. He had already acquired so high a reputation for his skill and judgment in the treatment of architectural subjects, that the service of his pencil was sought, to make us acquainted with the structures of the Moors in Spain, and to make drawings from, and adapt for the use of the engraver, many of the sketches furnished by travellers in Palestine, of the buildings and objects of interest published in the *Illustrations of the Bible*. These studies, and his journey to Spain and Morocco for his Spanish scenery, excited in him an irrepressible desire to visit the East. The drawings of the French Commission in Egypt had been declared very incorrect, and De Laborde's Petra was charged also with inaccuracy. To go and draw for himself scenes and objects of such intense interest could alone satisfy him; the result has been his richly stored portfolios, from which the subjects for his work have been selected.

Having made himself thoroughly acquainted with all matters requisite for the journey, and such works as were published on the countries and objects he was about to visit, and having prepared himself with letters and introductions, especially from the Foreign Office to Colonel Campbell, the Consul-General in Egypt and Syria, he left London August 31st, 1838, and reached Alexandria on the 24th of September following. Every facility was kindly and readily given by Colonel Campbell for the accomplishment of our artists objects. The Nile was at its height, and therefore visited at the most advantageous time. He ascended to Cairo, with introductions from Colonel Campbell, and there, by the aid of those to whom he had been recommended, Mr. Roberts was furnished with a guard to accompany him everywhere, and protect him from interruption or insult whilst sketching: he even obtained permission to enter every mosque he desired to visit, a privilege never before given to a Christian, but to which one condition was attached, that in the instruments he used in making his studies, for he was allowed to paint there, he was not to desecrate the mosque by the introduction and use of brushes made of hog's bristles.

From Cairo Mr. Roberts, with an Arab servant, ascended the Nile in a boat commanded by a captain with a crew of eight men, provisioned for three months. He was entirely master of the party, and carried the British flag at the mast head. He thus ascended to the second cataract, Wady Halfa, and before he returned to Cairo, had made drawings of almost every edifice from the extremity of Nubia to the Mediterranean.

While at Cairo, he made the acquaintance of M. Linant, who had been De Labordes' companion in his visit to Petra; he kindly showed Mr. Roberts the original sketches which had been made in that excursion, and thus added stimulants, which were unnecessary, to his undertaking the interesting journey to Wadi Mousa, or Petra. He immediately made preparations for crossing the desert by the route of the Israelities to Mount Sinai, by Akabah, and through the great valley of El Ghor to Petra, and thence to Hebron, instead of entering Palestine by El Arish and Gaza, as he had intended.

On February 8, 1839, having been joined by Mr. Pell and Mr. Kinnear (the latter of whom has since published an account of this journey), they assumed the Arab dress, and, with their servants well-armed, left Cairo, taking with them twenty-one camels, and escorted by nearly as many Bedouin Arabs of the tribe of the Beni Sa'ids.

On the 27th they reached the Fortress of Akabah, on the Red Sea; here they parted with the Arab tribe, hitherto their friends and guides, and put themselves under the escort of the tribe of Alloeens, who were to conduct them to Petra and thence to Hebron. On the 6th of March they reached Mount Hor, upon which rests the tomb of Aaron; at its base, deeply seated in its ravines and bounded by its precipitous sides and lofty peaks, lies the excavated city of Petra, the Idumea of the Greeks, the Edom of the prophet Jeremiah — the city of impregnable position, which gloried in its strength, but which strikes the traveller, who is fortunate enough to visit it, as an awful realization of the prophetic denunciations: *"Thy terribleness hath deceived thee, and the pride of thine heart, O thou that dwellest in the clefts of the rock, that holdest the height of the hill: though thou shouldest make thy nest as high as the eagle, I will bring thee down from thence, saith the Lord." (Jer 49:16)*

Mr. Roberts and his companions were the first who had been permitted to pitch their tents within Petra; this was the result of a long and violent altercation between the Arab tribe inhabiting Wady Mousa and the Alloeens, with whom an old grudge remained unsettled. At length a sufficient amount was agreed upon as a peace-offering for a truce, and the occupation of an encampment within the city for five days without molestation; during this time our artist, fortunately, worked incessantly on his studies, for on the fifth night the little party was assailed and some of their arms were carried off; but it was suspected by our travellers, that the attack of the Arabs of Wady Mousa was connived at by their guides, who were impatient to return; the next morning they struck their tents, and bade farewell to Petra, the wonder of the desert.

On the 16th, the party having reached Hebron, and learned that the plague had barred access to Jerusalem, proceeded to the coast, visiting Gaza, Askelon, and Jaffa; but being informed here that no recent case had occurred in the Holy City, and that the quarantine would shortly be removed, they set out for Jerusalem, and arrived there on the 29th of March, the day before Palm Sunday, a day held by the Christians in the East in great veneration. While at Jerusalem, Mr. Roberts received much kindness and assistance from the then governor, Achmet Aga, whom he accompanied with about four thousand Christian pilgrims to Jericho and the river Jordan. He afterwards visited the Dead Sea, the Lake of Tiberias, the sea coast and mountain range of Lebanon, and the ruins of Baalbec; such exertions, and the severe privations which he suffered on the journey, produced intermittent fever, which compelled him to abandon his projected excursions to Damascus and Palmyra. How entirely he had been devoted to the great objects he had proposed to himself before he left England, this work will abundantly prove. The extraordinary merit and interest of his drawings, when seen after his return, created a sensation not easily forgotten; the fidelity of his accurate pencil, his skillful and rigid adherence to the truth of costume, his attention to just and characteristic effect, were acknowledged by all travellers and artists competent to judge. The demand for his work sprang out of the interest thus excited. Commissions from royalty and the chief patrons of art crowded upon him for pictures from the subjects he had studied in the East, and his contemporaries in art acknowledged his merits by the honour of electing him into the Royal Academy.

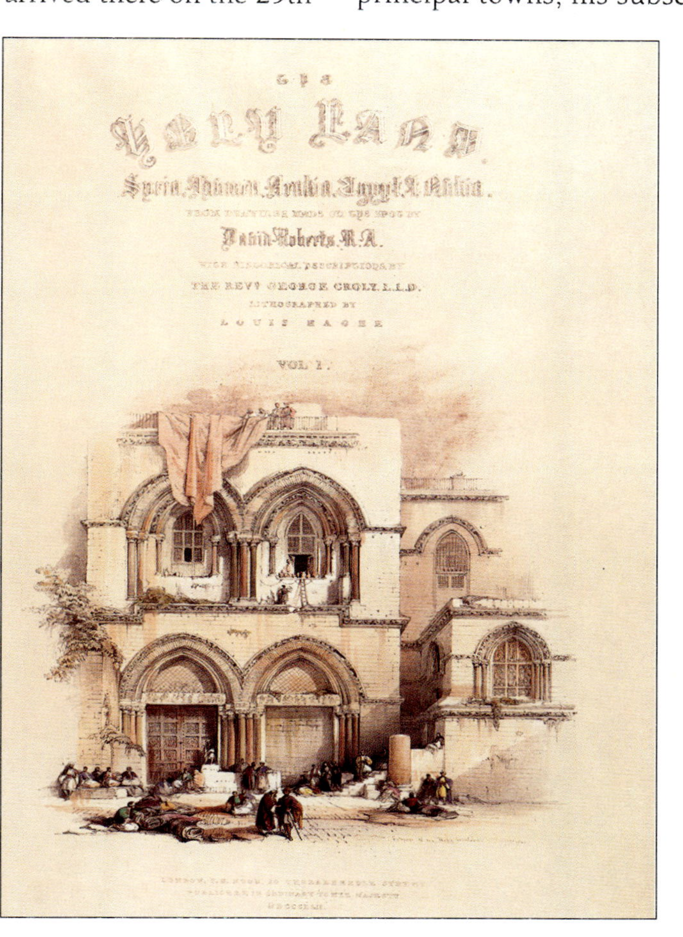

Publication of *The Holy Land*

The publishing of his great work *The Holy Land*, caused David Roberts many unpleasant moments in dealing with some publishers, but at last he found Mr. Francis G. Moon, to whom he offered the work, as mentioned in his Journal: ". . . I made him acquainted with all these circumstances, and he at once agreed to bring out the work in the manner I had proposed. . . . This was a great risk on the publishers' part: but by exhibiting the drawings in London and other principal towns, his subscription list in May 1841 was nearly double Murray's estimated costs. . . . Before the drawings were shown to the public, they were submitted to the Queen, to the Archbishops of York and Canterbury, and to the Bishop of London, who all subscribed for the work, the Queen graciously allowing it to be dedicated to her. . . ." The work was received with great enthusiasm, as described by E.A. Abbey: ". . . the first studies ever made to give the portraiture of scenes of historical and religious interest. They were faithful and laborious beyond any outlines from nature. In point of bulk and ambition, Roberts' *Holy Land* was one of the most important and elaborate ventures of nineteenth-century publishing, and it was the apotheosis of the tinted lithograph. . . ." On the quality of the work, David Roberts himself gave his own appreciation of the lithographer, Louis Haghe, who ". . . not only duly surpassed himself, but all that has hitherto been done of a similar nature. He has rendered the views in a style clear, simple and unlabored, with a masterly vigour and boldness which none but a painter like him could have transferred to stone." (from the *First Edition*, London, 1842.)

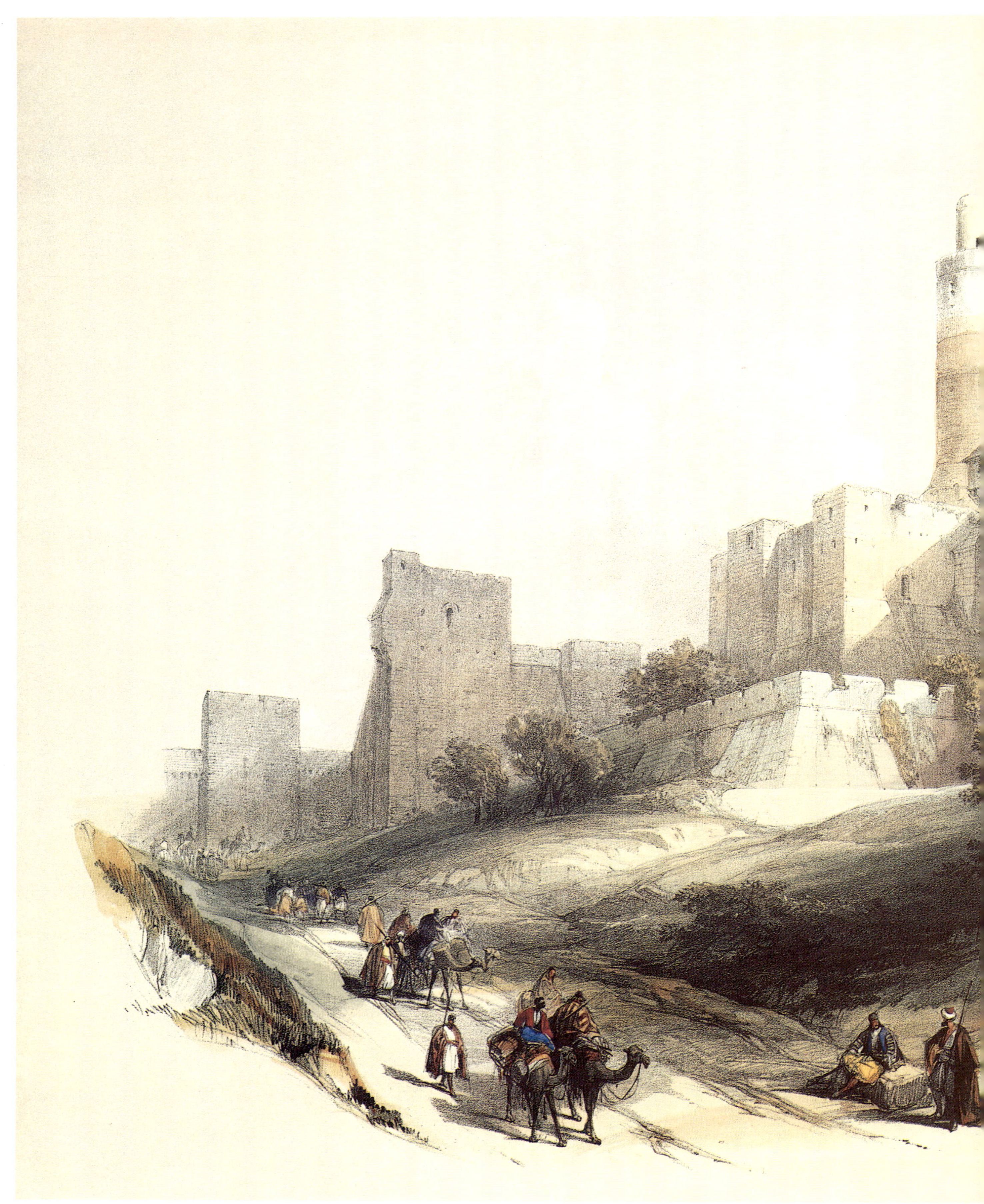

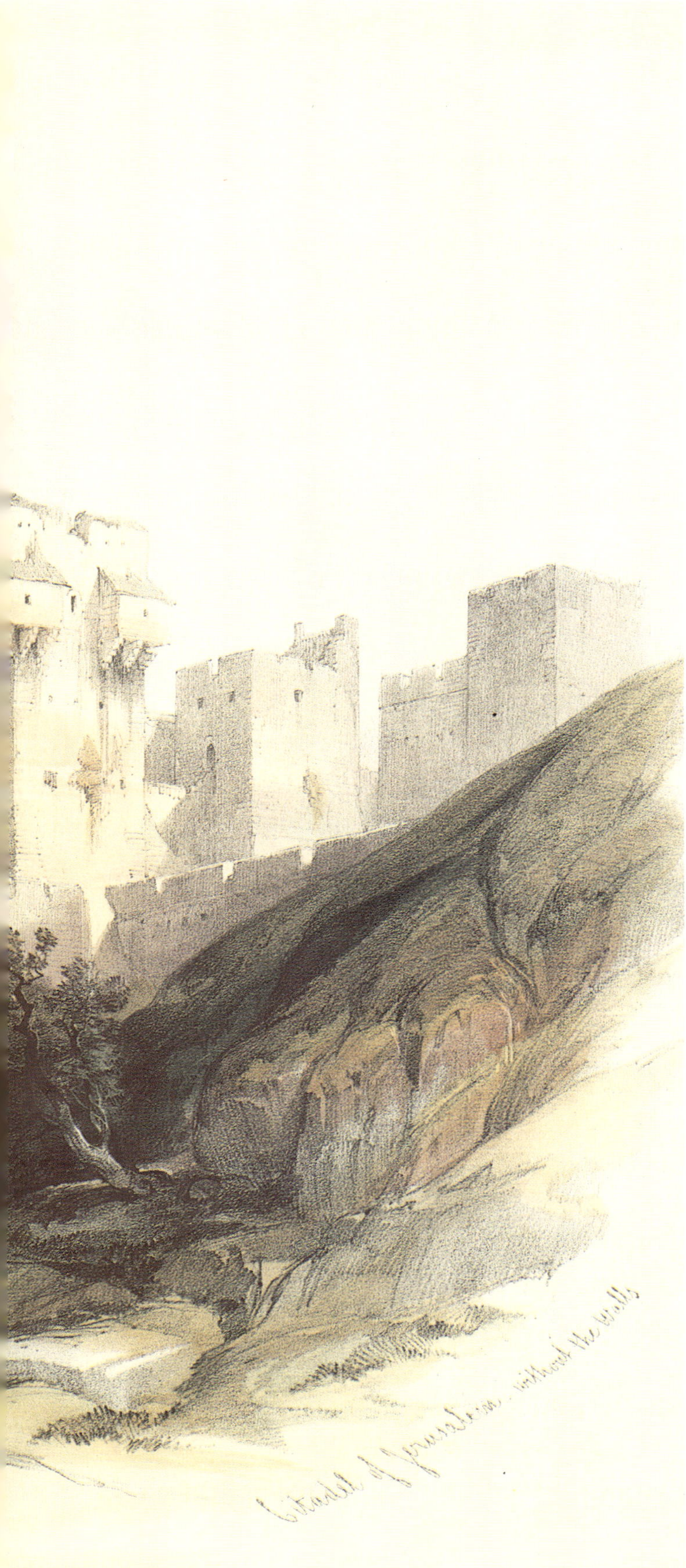

Jerusalem, the Tower of David

So David dwelt in the fort, and called it the city of David. And David built round about from Millo and inward (2 Sam. 5:9).

The Citadel of modern Jerusalem, an irregular assemblage of square towers, lies on the northwestern part of Sion, to the South of the Jaffa Gate. A sloping bulwark protects the towers, and bears evident marks of remote antiquity — it is thought to be of the time of Hadrian. Some of the stones of the north-eastern tower are 12' long by 3' 5" broad.

Jerusalem, the Entrance to the Citadel

And David went on, and grew great, and the Lord God of hosts [was] with him (2 Sam. 5:10).

The chief interest connected with the modern walls is that they generally exhibit evidence of their having been raised on the site of others, going back to the ages of the Roman conquest, of the Idumaean dynasty, or perhaps even of the reign of Solomon, the last, a time all whose recollections are hallowed to the Jew, and not less to the Christian.

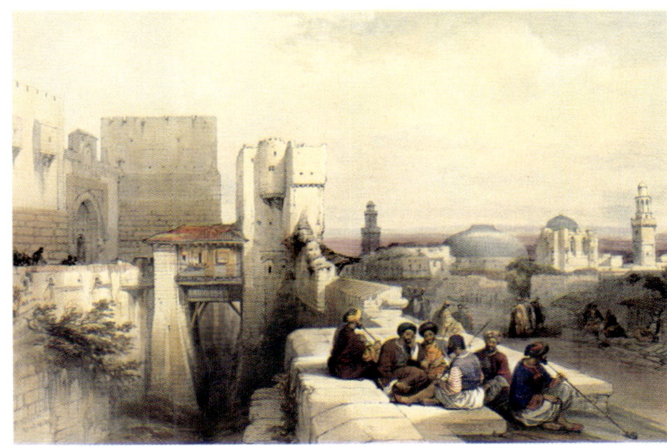

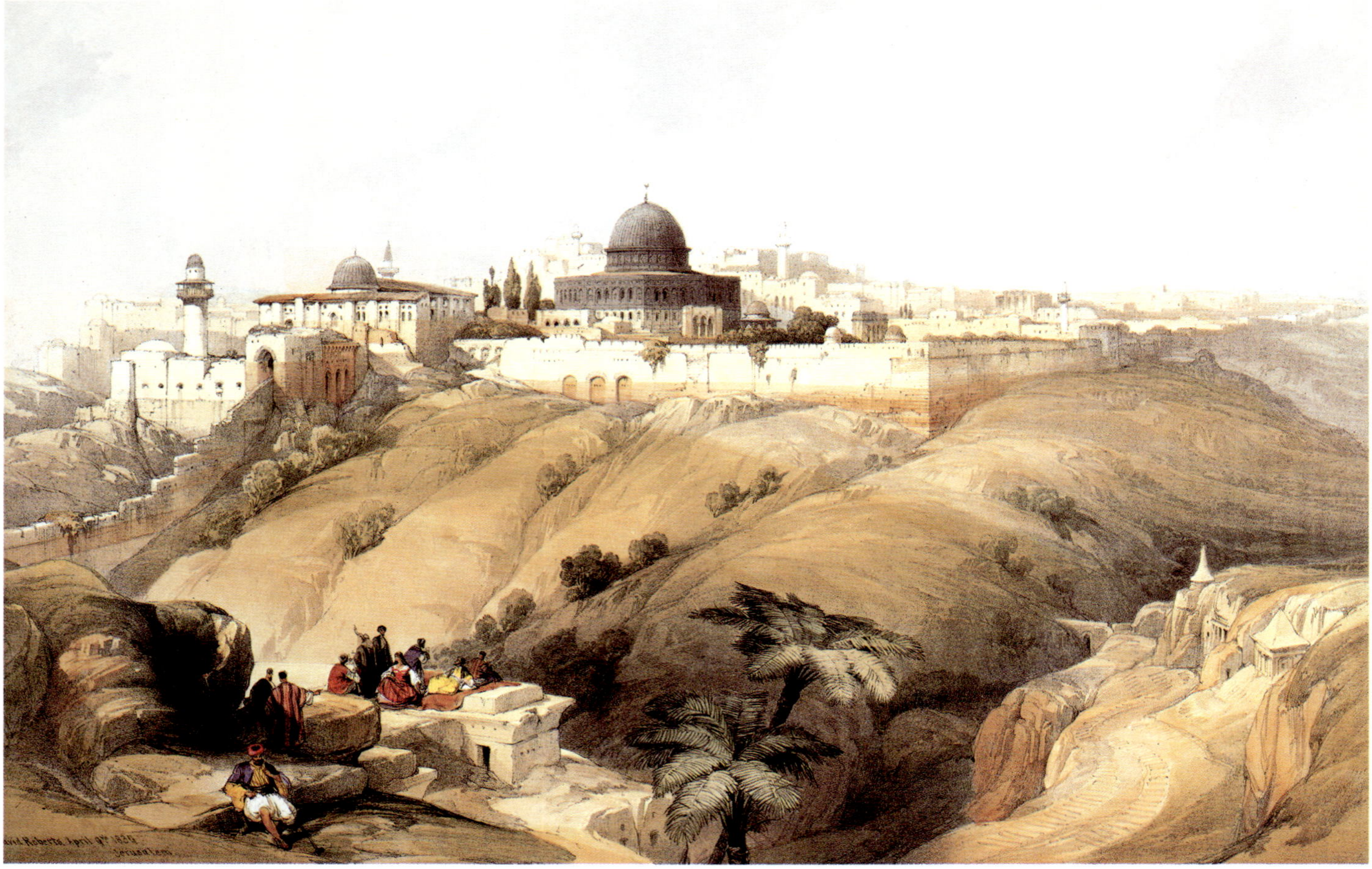

Jerusalem, the Church of the Purification

And the angel came in unto her, and said, Hail, [thou that art] highly favoured, the Lord [is] with thee: blessed [art] thou among women (Luke 1:28). An inquiry has been long on foot among the intelligent investigators of the Holy Land, for the site of the great church built by Justinian, in honor of the Virgin Mary in the sixth century. Procopius states it to have been erected on the loftiest hill of the city: as there was not enough space for its intended magnitude, the architect was compelled to raise a wall with arched vaults from the valley to support the southeast part of the edifice. The only fabric whose site corresponds with this description is the Mosque El-Aksa.

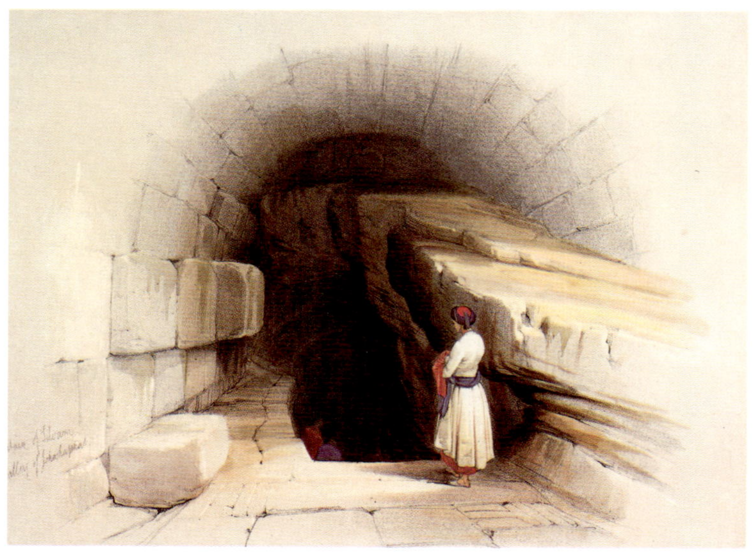

The Pool of Siloah
(The Upper Fountain of Siloah)

But the gate of the fountain repaired Shallun the son of Colhozeh, the ruler of part of Mizpah; he built it, and covered it, and set up the doors thereof, the locks thereof, and the bars thereof, and the wall of the pool of Siloah by the king's garden, and unto the stairs that go down from the city of David (Neh. 3:15).

Siloah consists of two basins or fountains, the upper one of which is a fissure in the solid rock. A flight of steps leads down on the inside to the water, and close at hand on the outside is the reservoir. This seems to be generally acknowledged as "Siloah's brook that flowed fast by the oracle of God." The drawing of the water from Siloah in the Feast of Tabernacles became a remarkable ceremonial in the latter ages of Judea.

Jerusalem, Site of the Temple

And the house, when it was in building, was built of stone made ready before it was brought thither: so that there was neither hammer nor axe [nor] any tool of iron heard in the house, while it was in building (1 Kings 6:7).

This fine monument, the Mosque of Omar, stands on Mount Moriah the ancient site of the temple. For many hundreds of years pilgrims have come to this holy place in Jerusalem regarded as the center of the world. The group consists of Greek Christians praying towards the Holy Sepulchre. They stand on a terrace of the dilapidated Church of St. Anna. The Mount of Olives is partially seen to the left.

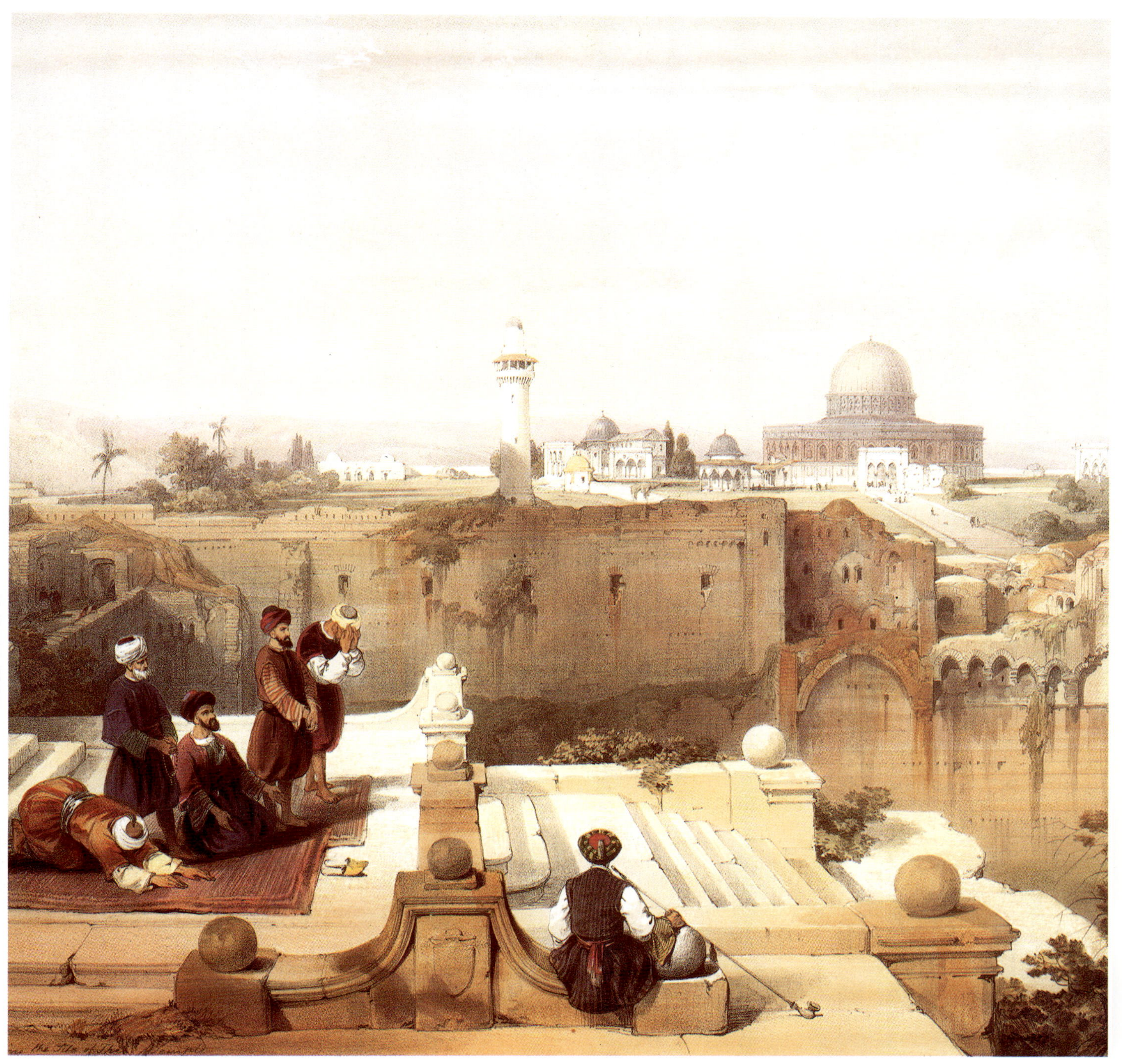

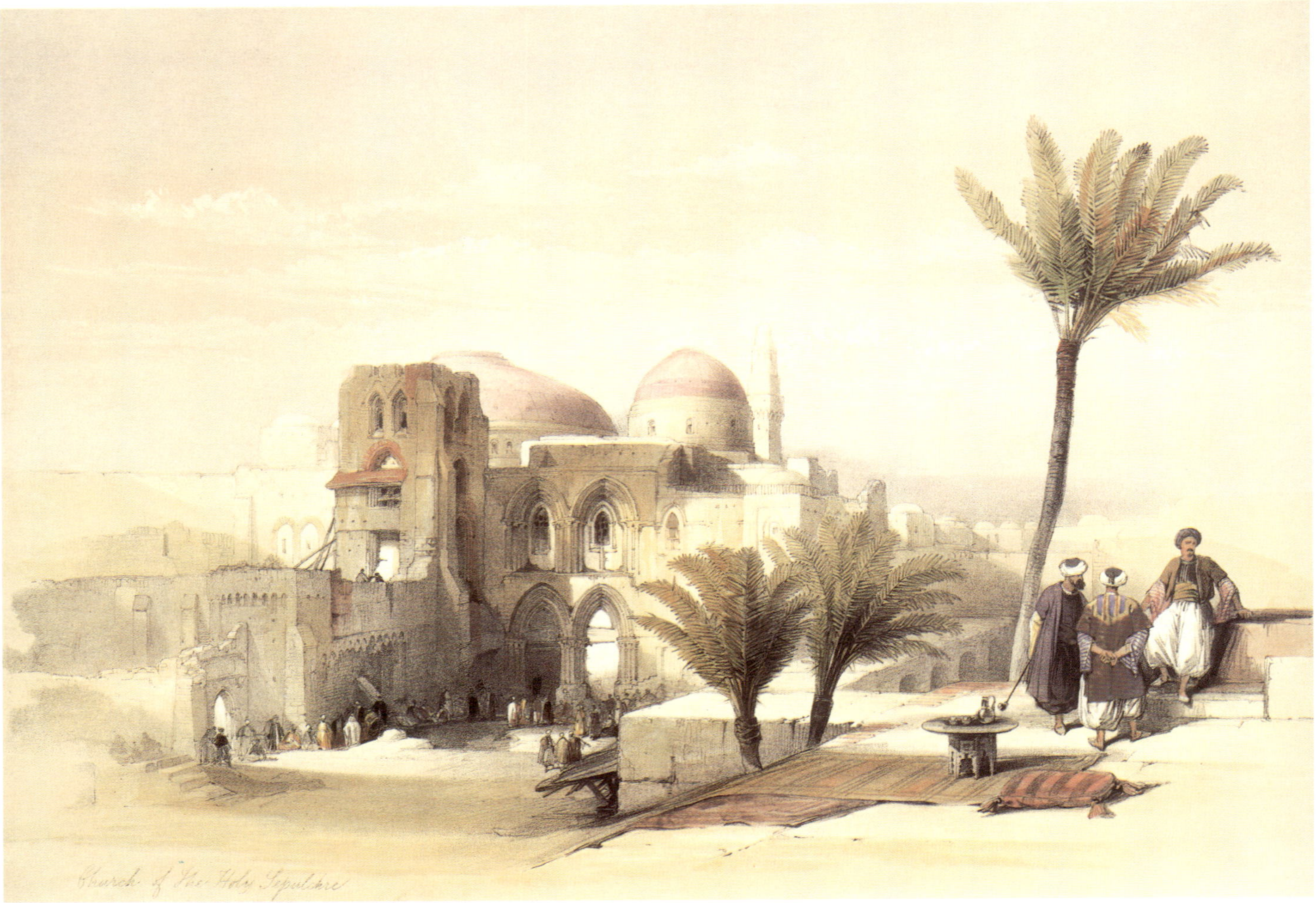

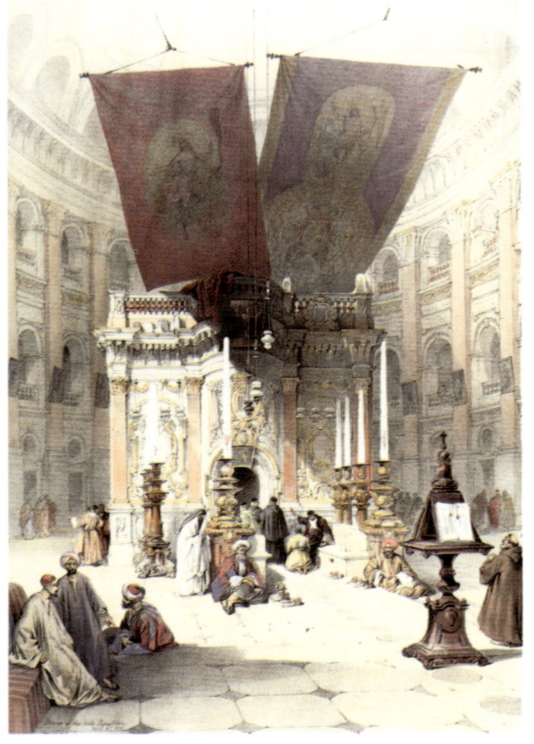

Jerusalem, the Holy Sepulchre

Remember the word that I said unto you, The servant is not greater than his lord. If they have persecuted me, they will also persecute you; if they have kept my saying, they will keep yours also (John 5:20).

"The first and most interesting object within the walls of the Holy City, the spot to which every pilgrim directs his steps, is the Holy Sepulchre: but the traveller finds his expectation strangely disappointed when, approaching the hallowed tomb, he sees around him the tottering houses of a ruined city, and is conducted to the door of a gigantic church." The ruined tower to the left was anciently the belfry.

Jerusalem, the Shrine of the Holy Sepulchre

The first aspect of the exterior is striking. It is a vast and splendid monument, imposing, and rich for the time at which it was erected. It is true that it is not the church built by the mother of Constantine; but in its rebuilding . . . the ornaments of the Byzantine architecture have been preserved, and, with those of the Greek and Eastern, form a noble and most picturesque temple. . . . The heart, and the understanding too, may rest fully contented with the fact, that whether within or without this dome, here trod our Lord.

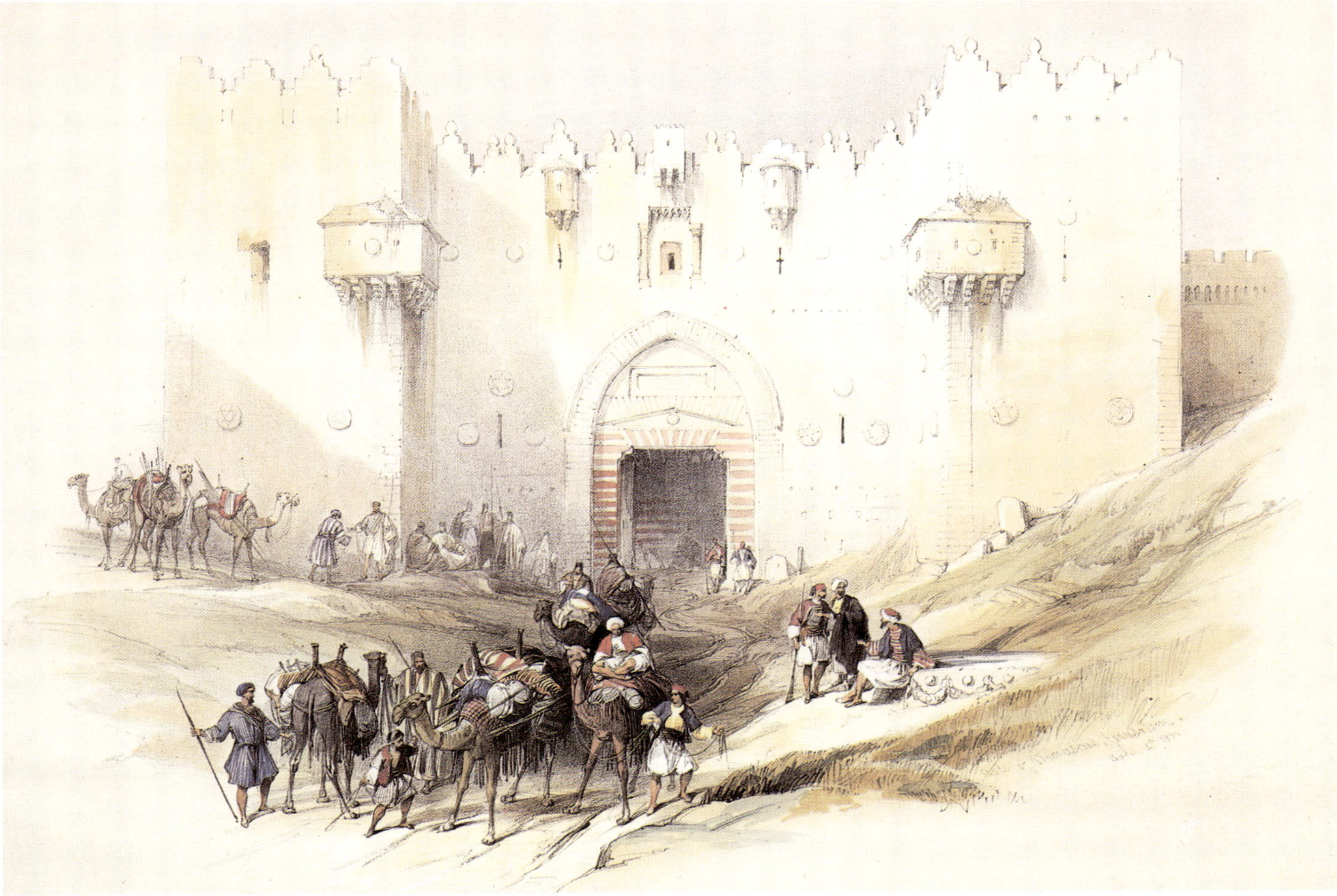

Jerusalem, Damascus Gate

Therefore thy gates shall be open continually; they shall not be shut day nor night; that [men] may bring unto thee the forces of the Gentiles, and [that] their kings [may be] brought (Isaiah 60:11).

"The walls of Jerusalem are chiefly modern and Saracenic, but are built evidently on the site of more ancient walls, raised in the time of the Crusaders, and those, not improbably, formed of the material of others still more ancient." The Damascus Gate built by the Sultan Suleiman the Magnificent in the 16th century looks to the north. Camels were the main form of transport, and there was a constant stream of traffic on this great northern highway leading to Nablus and Damascus .

Jerusalem, the Golden Gate

Then said the Lord unto me; This gate shall be shut, it shall not be opened, and no man shall enter in by it; because the Lord, the God of Israel, hath entered in by it, therefore it shall be shut (Ezek. 44:2). This is a massive structure — a double gateway. After the second revolt in A.D. 136, Hadrian built a new city, Aelia, and raised a temple to Jupiter. The style of the Golden Gate refers it to this period. The external front and arches are of Roman origin, and of the interior it is evident that **"a central row of noble Corinthian columns and a groined roof, had once formed a stately portico of Roman workmanship."**

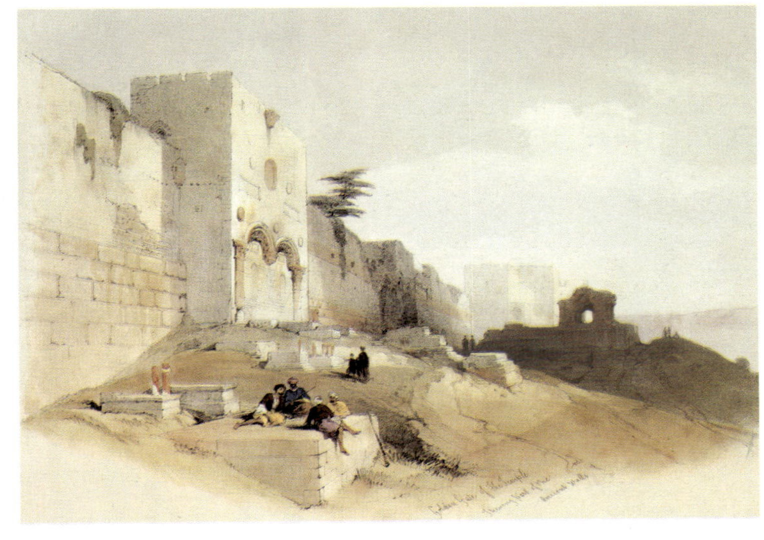

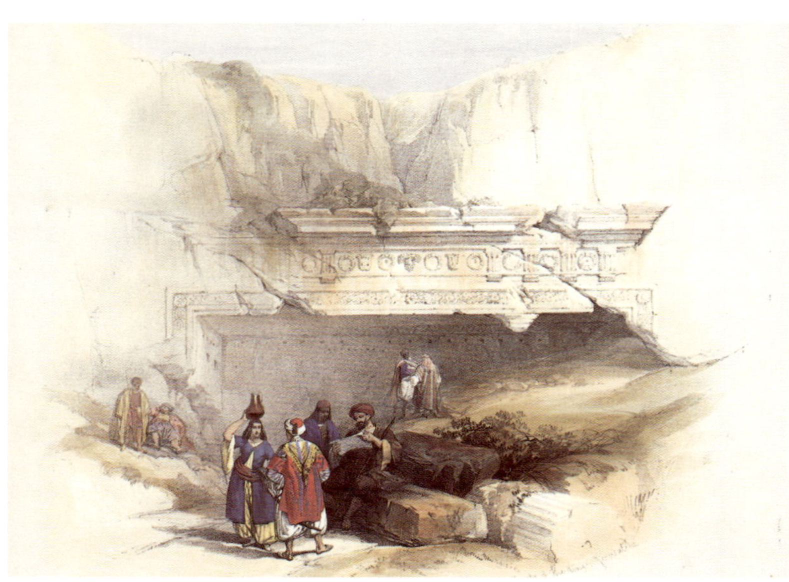

Jerusalem, the Pillar of Absalom

And they took Absalom, and cast him into a great pit in the wood, and laid a very great heap of stones upon him: and all Israel fled every one to his tent (2 Sam. 18:17).

Now Absalom in his lifetime had taken and reared up for himself a pillar, which is in the king's dale: for he said, I have no son to keep my name in remembrance: and he called the pillar after his own name: and it is called unto this day, Absalom's place.

Tomb of the Kings

This remarkable sepulchre is the finest relic of its kind in the neighborhood of Jerusalem. The weight of evidence inclines to its being the tomb of Helena, Queen of Adiabené, who had become a convert to Judaism.

Jerusalem, the Pool of Bethesda

For an angel went down at a certain season into the pool, and troubled the water: whosoever then first after the troubling of the water stepped in was made whole of whatsoever disease he had (John 5:4).

The eagerness of the early monks to give scriptural names to every prominent feature of Jerusalem has affixed the title "Pool of Bethesda" to the reservoir on the north of the great mosque.

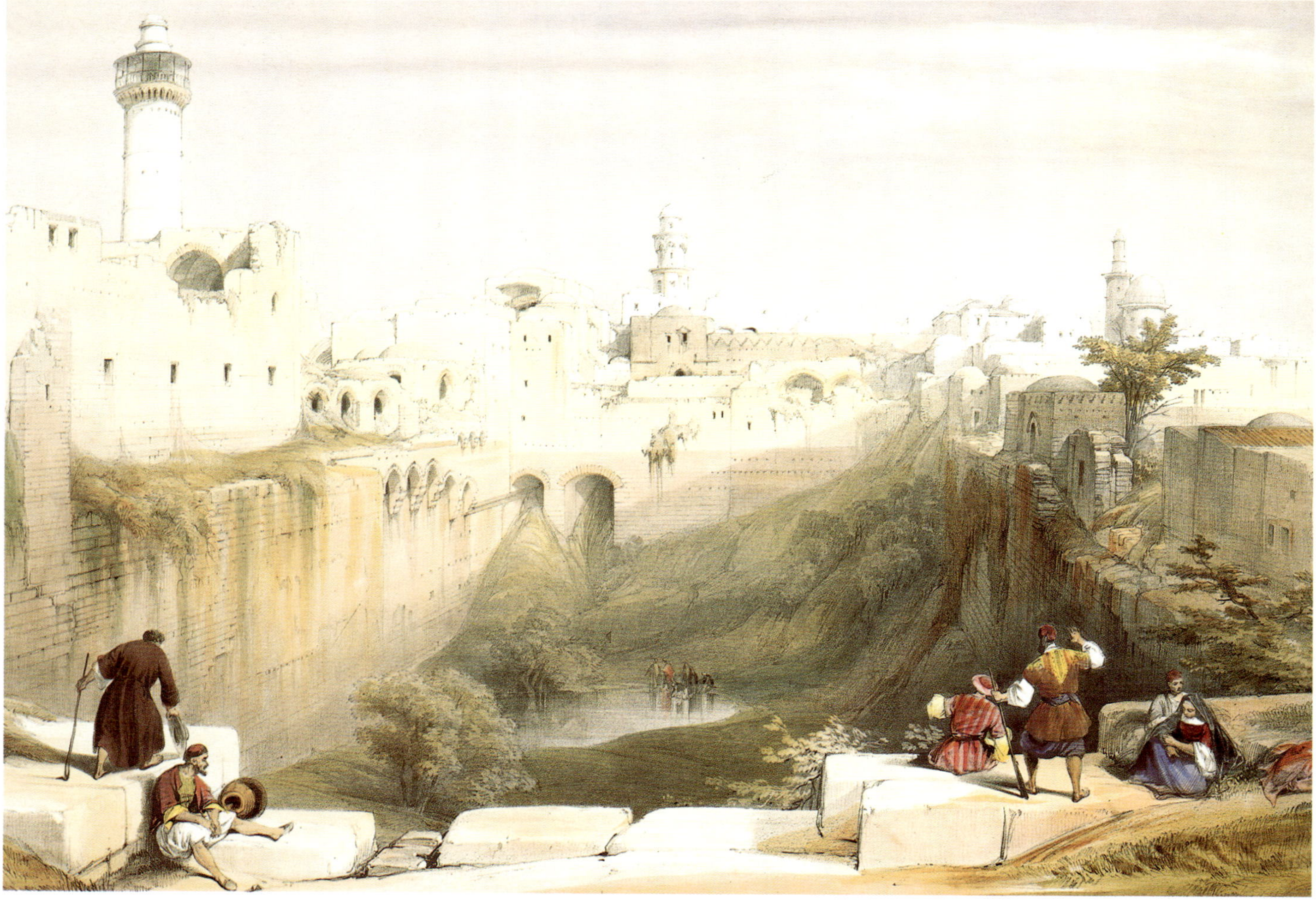

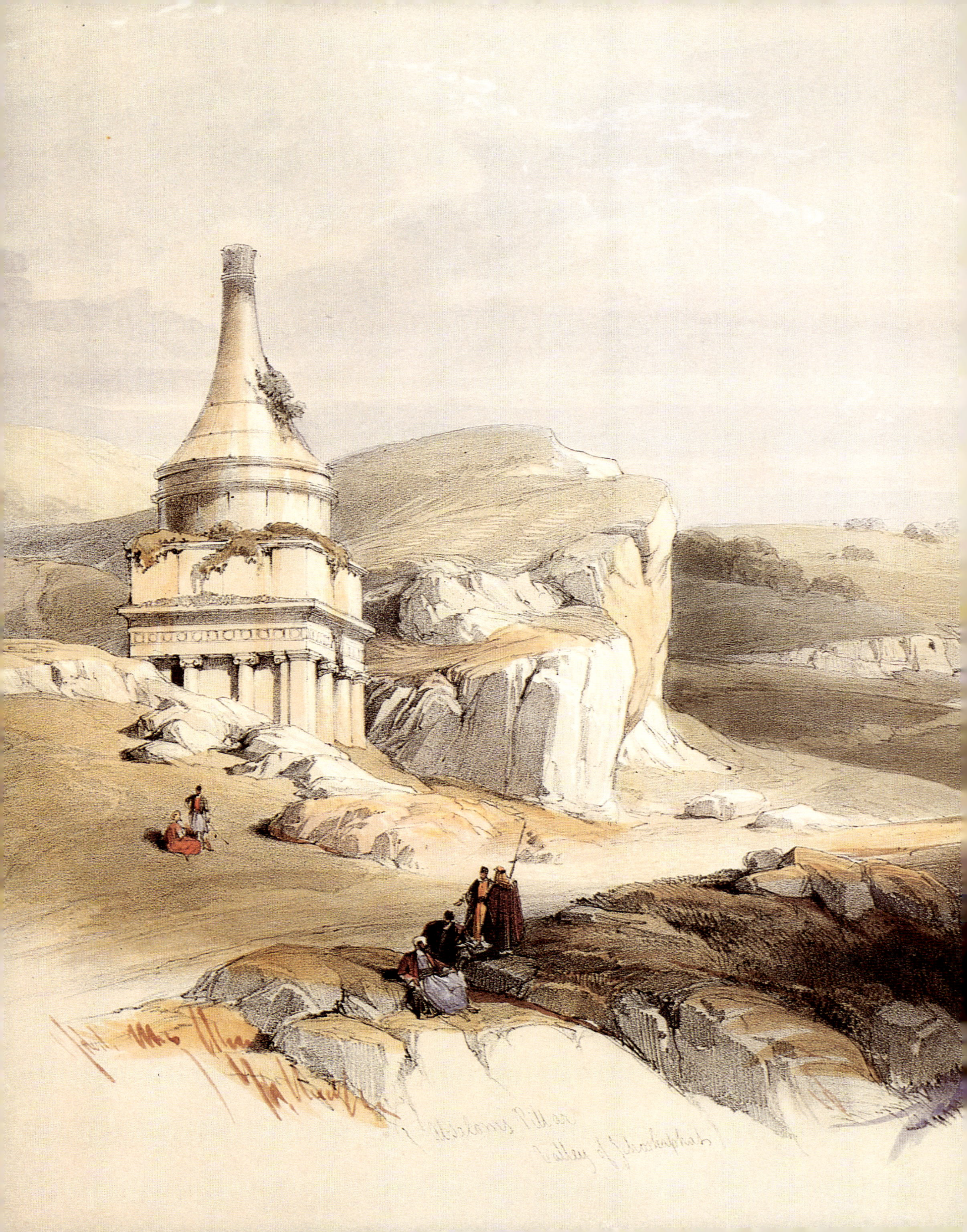
Absaloms Pillar
Valley of Jehoshaphat

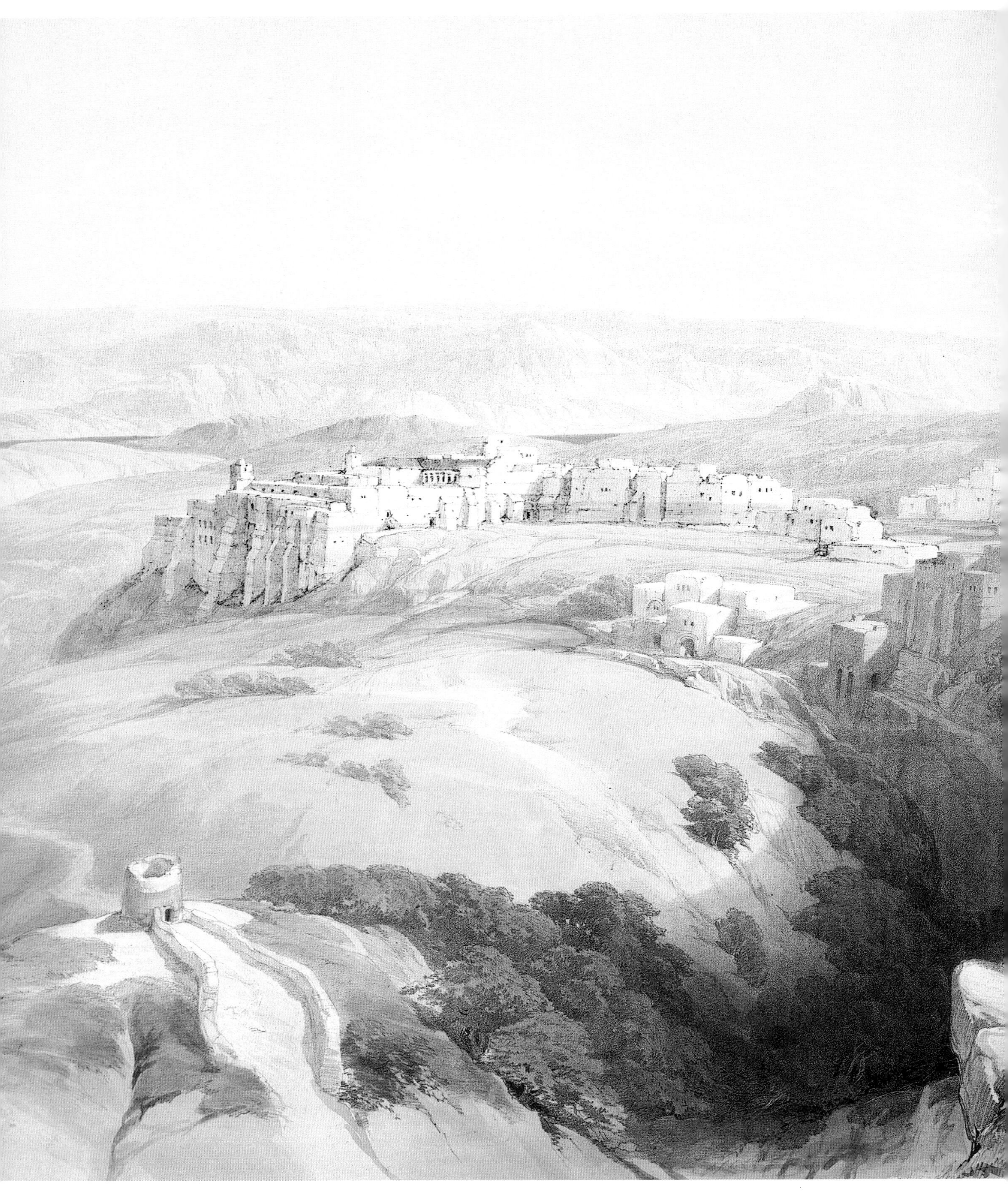

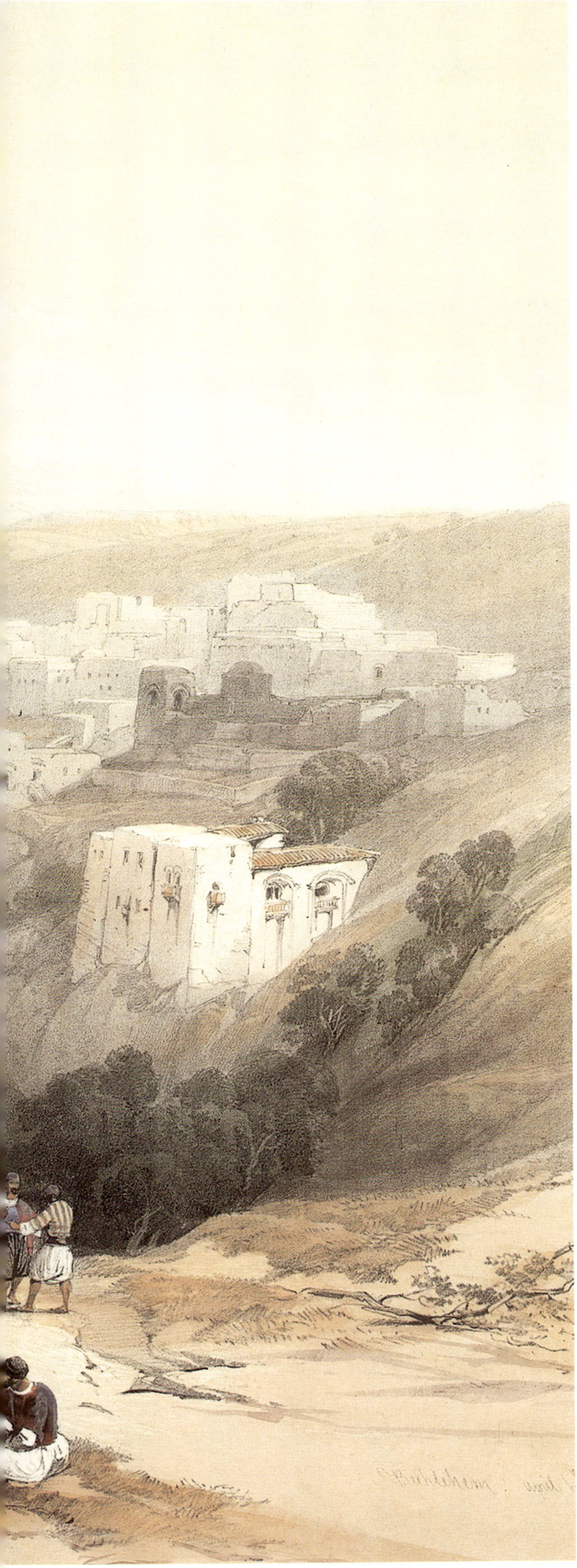

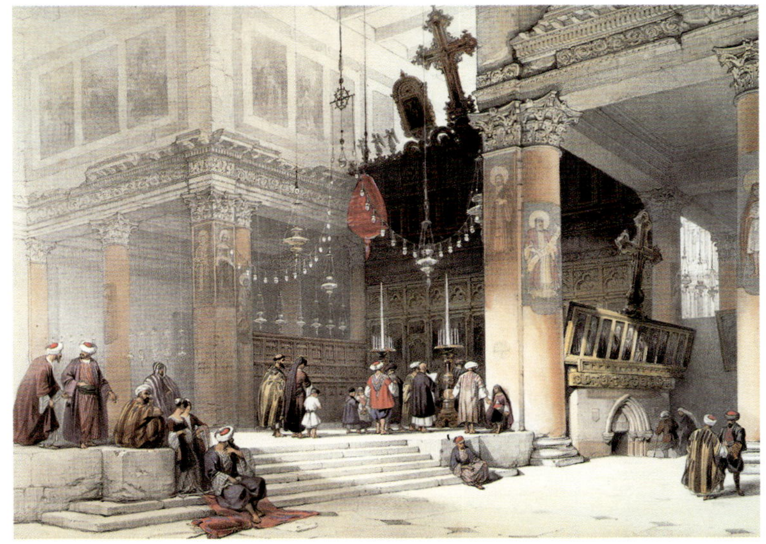

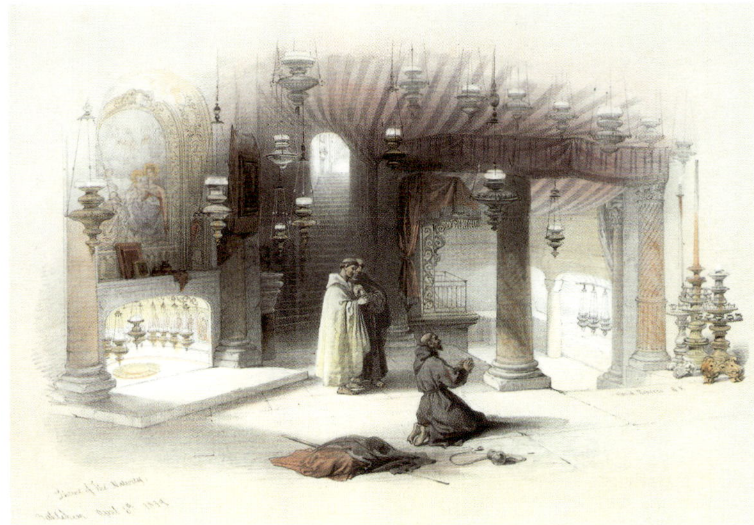

Bethlehem – the Shrine of the Nativity

But thou, Bethlehem Ephratah, [though] thou be little among the thousands of Judah, [yet] out of thee shall he come forth unto me [that is] to be ruler in Israel; whose goings forth [have been] from of old, from everlasting (Mic. 5:2).

This chamber, partly an excavation in the limestone, lies directly under the church built by Queen Helena. . . . On the right are three lamps suspended over the manger . . . opposite this the altar . . . said by the monks to mark the place where the Magi knelt to make their offerings. On the left is a semicircular recess. A glory represents the star which guided the Magi.

Bethlehem

The village lies about two hours distance from Jerusalem. The surrounding country — though hilly — is fertile and well-cultivated. In the distance are seen the hills of Moab, and below them a glimpse of the Dead Sea. In the interval between the Greek Convent and the mountain border of the Dead Sea rises a hill, named the Hill of the Franks, from a legend of the Crusades.

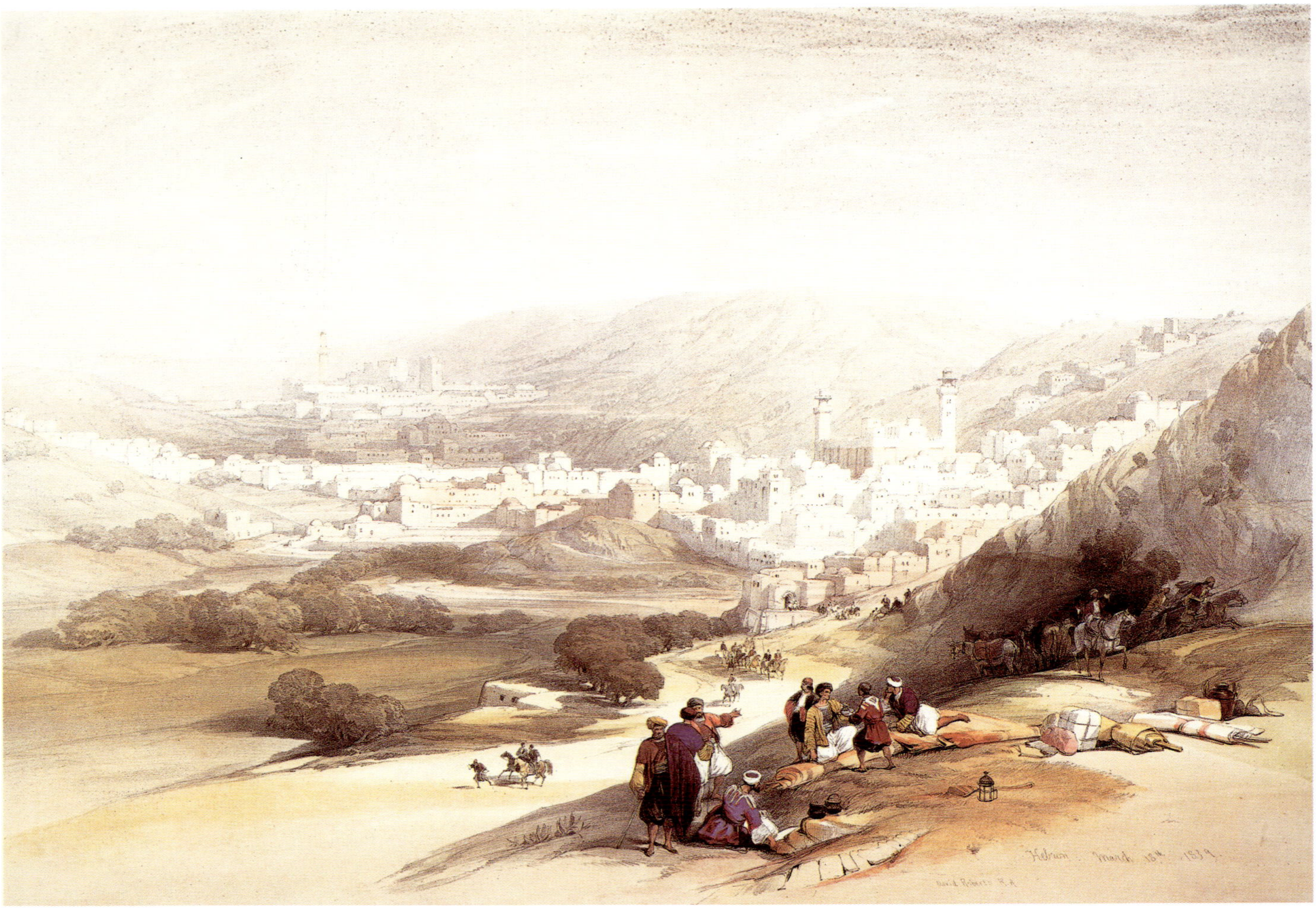

Hebron

So all the elders of Israel came to the king to Hebron; and king David made a league with them in Hebron before the Lord: and they anointed David king over Israel (2 Sam. 5:3).

Hebron is one of the most memorable sites of Palestine. It is one of the most ancient cities in the world. The artist describes Hebron: **"On turning the side of a hill, the little town of Hebron burst upon us. . . . Its situation is beautiful, and the houses glittering in the noon-day sun had a look of English cleanliness after the wretched hovels of Egypt. The children who came out to meet us were among the most beautiful I had ever seen."**

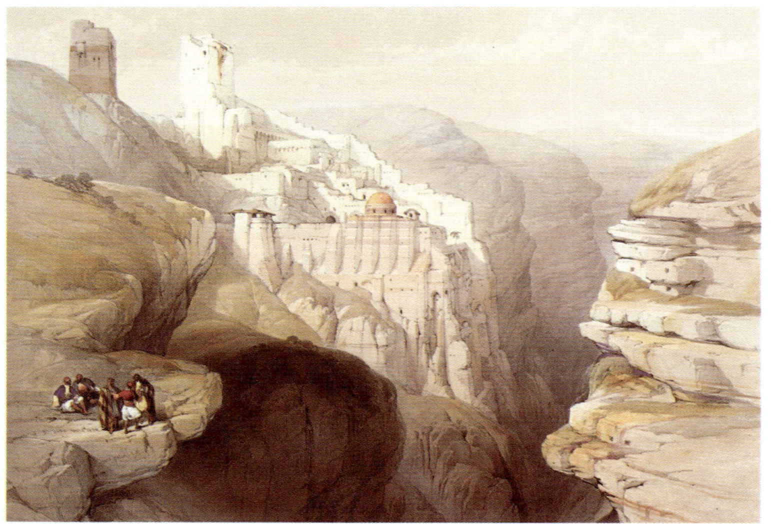

The Wilderness of Ein Gedi and the Convent of Mar Saba

O God, you are my God, earnestly I seek you; my soul thirsts for you, my body longs for you, in a dry and weary land where there is no water. I have seen you in the sanctuary and beheld your power and your glory (Ps. 63:1-2).

The Convent of St. Saba is about four leagues to the south-east of Jerusalem. The surrounding country is desert. The entrance doors are low, narrow and formed of iron or very thick wood. The monks pay and keep a regular guard of Arabs at the principal entrance; and in one of the towers a sentinel is constantly posted, to announce the approach of travelers or of Bedouins.

Lydda

And it came to pass, as Peter passed throughout all quarters, he came down also to the saints which dwelt at Lydda. And there he found a certain man named Aeneas (Acts 9:32).

This village, now known as Loud'h or Ludd, and once bearing the name of Diospolis, was originally of considerable importance. Built by the Benjamites and inhabited by them after their exile, it was transferred by Demetrius Nicator from Samaria to Judea. In the period following the death of Julius Caesar the city was seized, and its inhabitants sold into slavery. In the history of the New Testament it was the scene of a miracle.

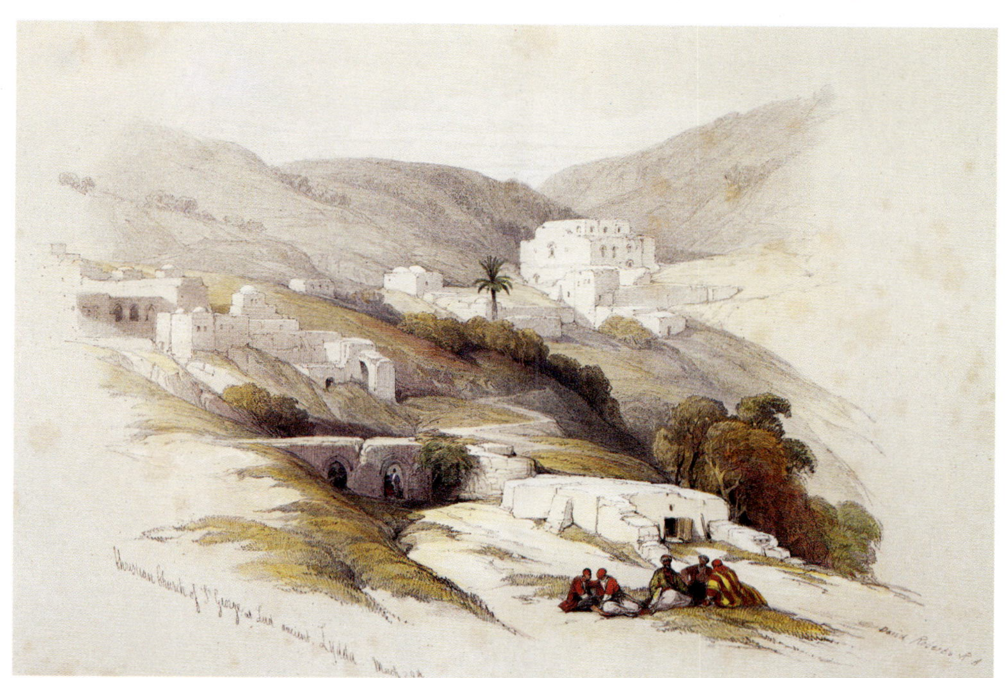

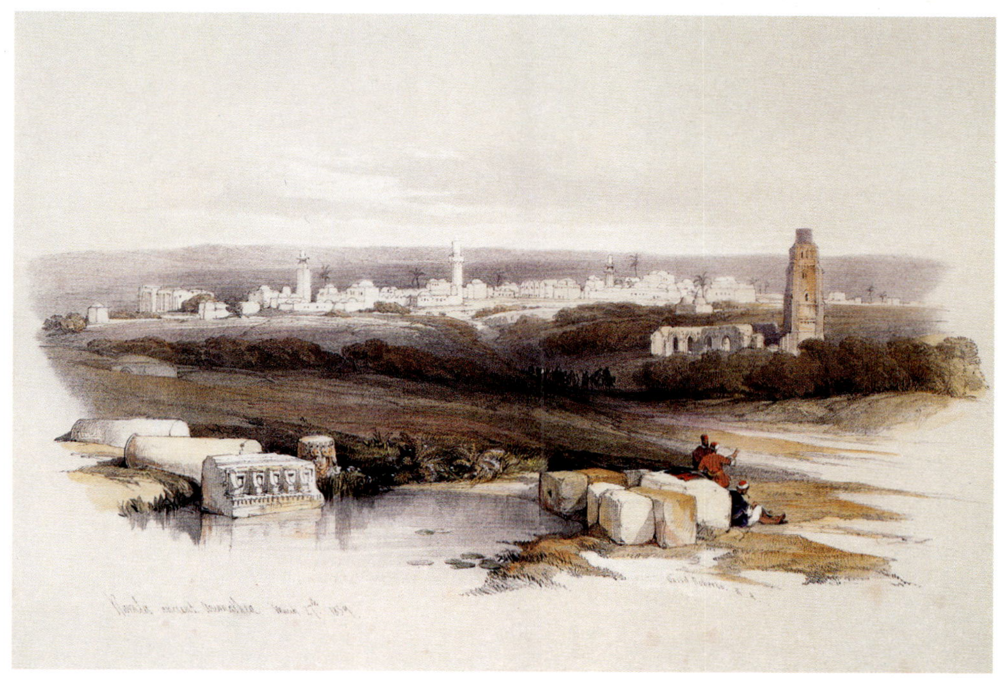

Ramla

And, behold, [there was] a man named Joseph, a counsellor; [and he was] a good man, and a just: (The same had not consented to the counsel and deed of them;) [he was] of Arimathaea, a city of the Jews: who also himself waited for the kingdom of God (Luke 23:50).

On the strength of a more than doubtful tradition, this town has been long regarded as the Arimathea of Scripture. It lies on the eastern side of a broad, low swell in the sandy plain, from which it has obviously taken its present name (Er-ramlah, the sand). Ramla has been rescued from the general decay of the seashore towns by the annual passage of the Great Caravan between Damascus and Egypt. The town contains several mosques and the largest Latin convent in Palestine.

The River Jordan, (the Immersion of the Pilgrims)

And Joshua said, Hereby ye shall know that the living God [is] among you. . . . Behold, the ark of the covenant of the Lord of all the earth passeth over before you into Jordan (Josh. 3:10-11).

In this view, Achmed Aga, the governor of Jerusalem, with part of his Arab guard occupy the foreground. "**As we approached the brink of the river, a general rush took place . . . even the camels, though heavily loaded, could scarcely be restrained. The governor's carpets were spread on a high bank close to the river, where we could command a view of the entire scene; the military band and colors were brought round him and seats were assigned to our party.**" One of the achievements is to be the first to plunge into the stream.

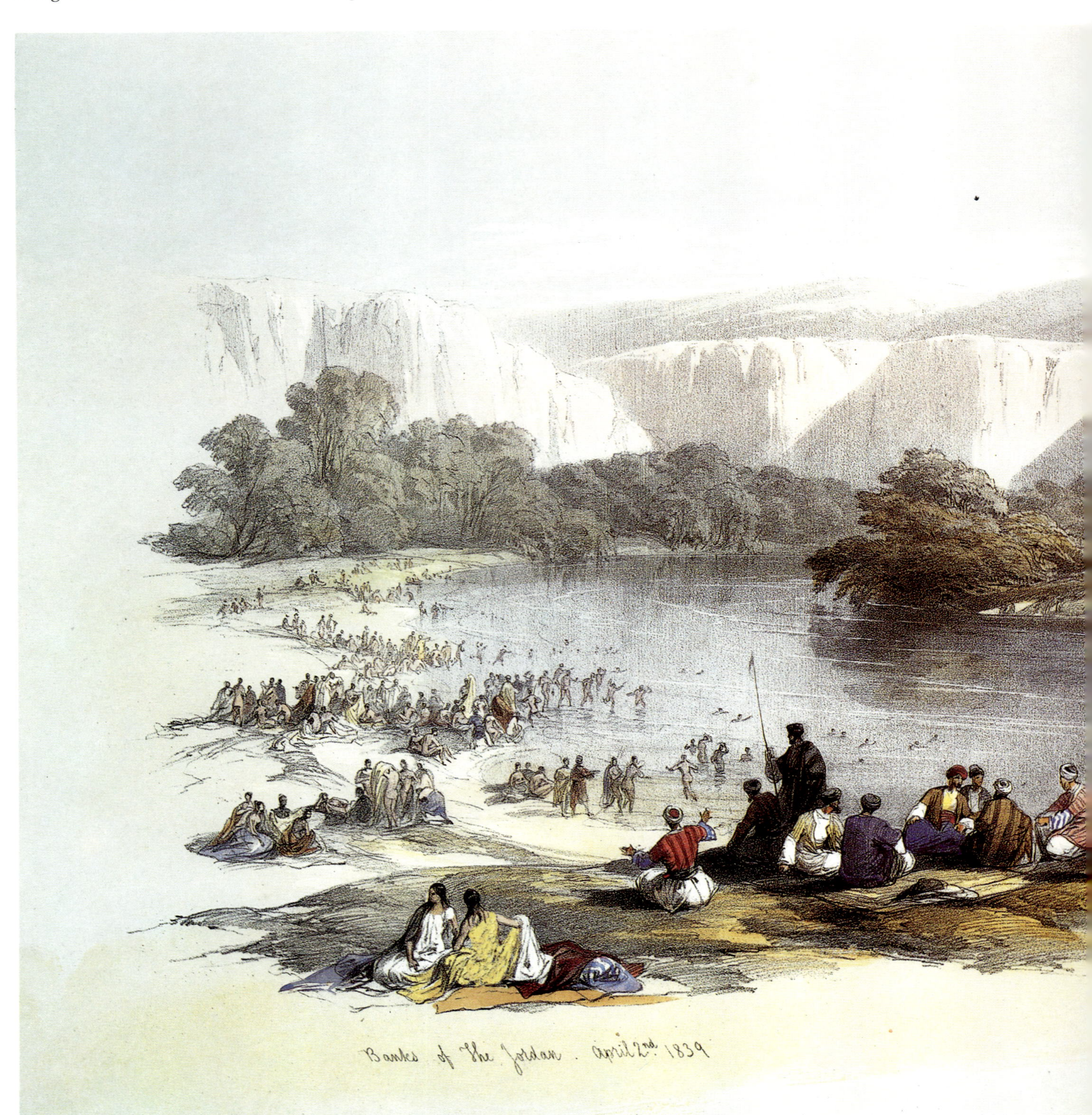

Jericho

In his days did Hiel the Bethelite build Jericho: he laid the foundation thereof in Abiram his firstborn, and set up the gates thereof in his youngest [son] Segub, according to the word of the Lord, which he spake by Joshua the son of Nun (1 Kings 16:34).

"Our encampment was soon buried in sleep as the night came on, though occasionally I caught sounds of the song and the dance, either from the tents of the pilgrims or our Arab guard. The night was one of the most beautiful which I had seen even in the country, and the moon was reflected in all its brightness on the silent waters of the Dead Sea." The climate of Jericho is excessively hot and nor is this surprising, when it is considered that the caldron of the Dead Sea and the Valley of the Jordan lie several hundred feet below the level of the ocean, and nearly three thousand feet lower than Jerusalem.

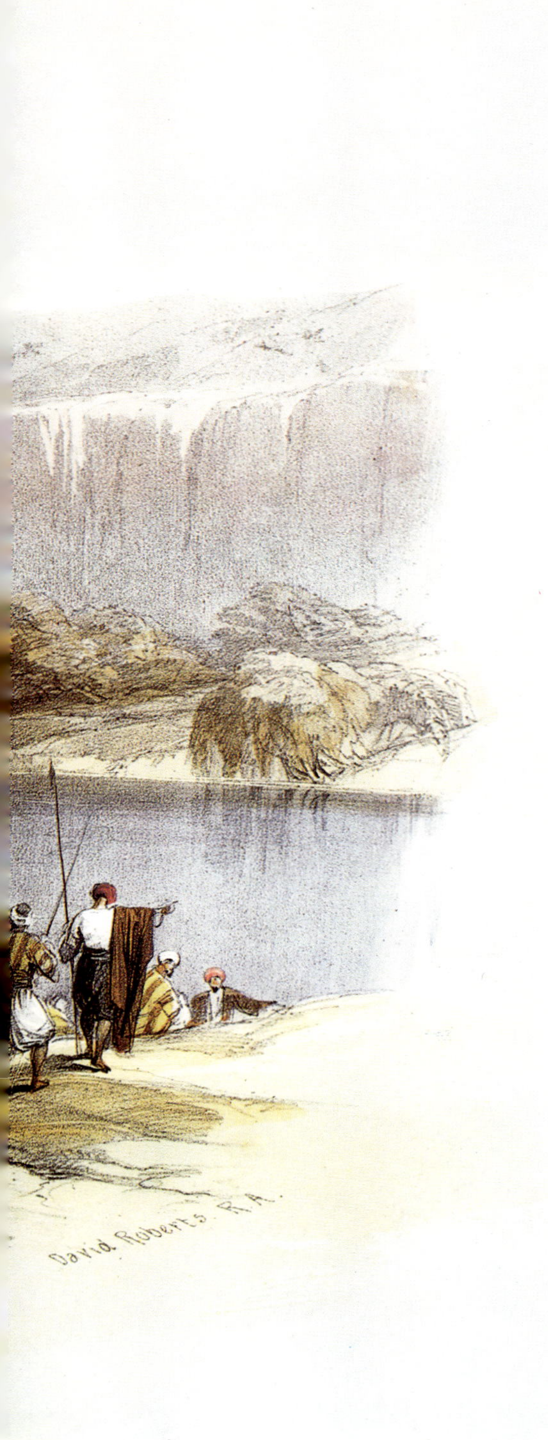

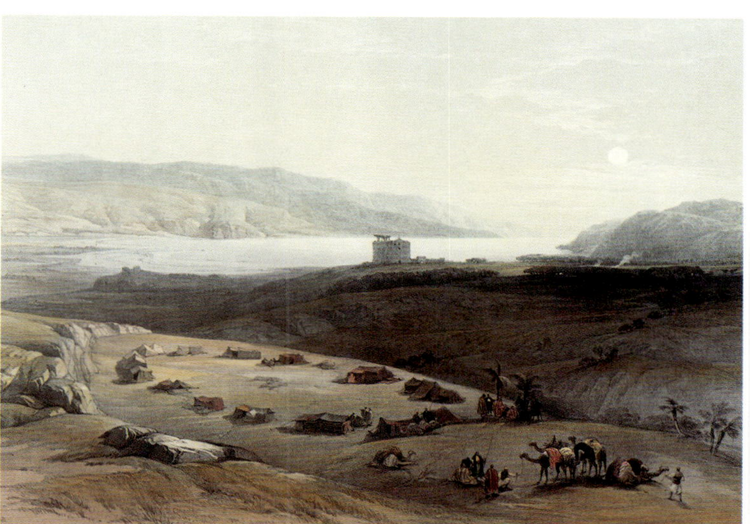

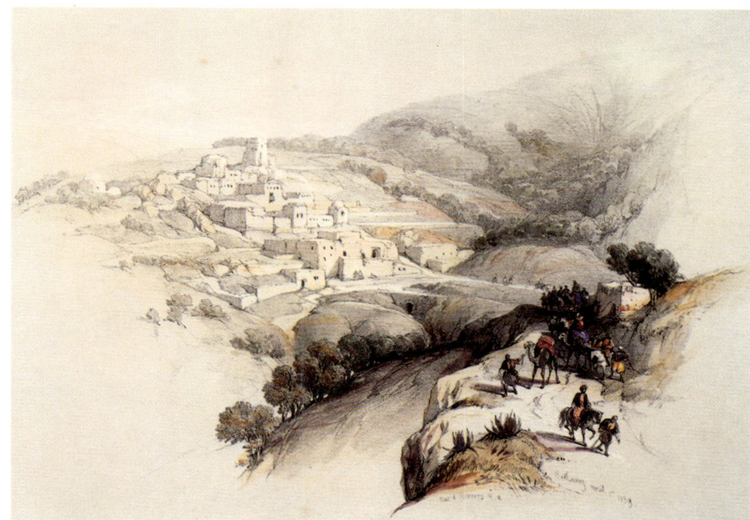

Bethany

Now a certain [man] was sick, [named] Lazarus, of Bethany, the town of Mary and her sister Martha (John 11:1-2).

Bethany was the well-known scene of one of the mightiest miracles of our Lord — that restoration of Lazarus to life, by which he especially proclaimed his power over the grave, in the immediate presence of Jerusalem. Bethany, it being now called El-Aziriyeh, from El-Azir (Arab. Lazarus). The sepulchre is a deep vault excavated in the limestone rock, in the middle of the village; this spot has been a place of remarkable veneration in very early ages as the site of a church, successive monasteries also having been built over it.

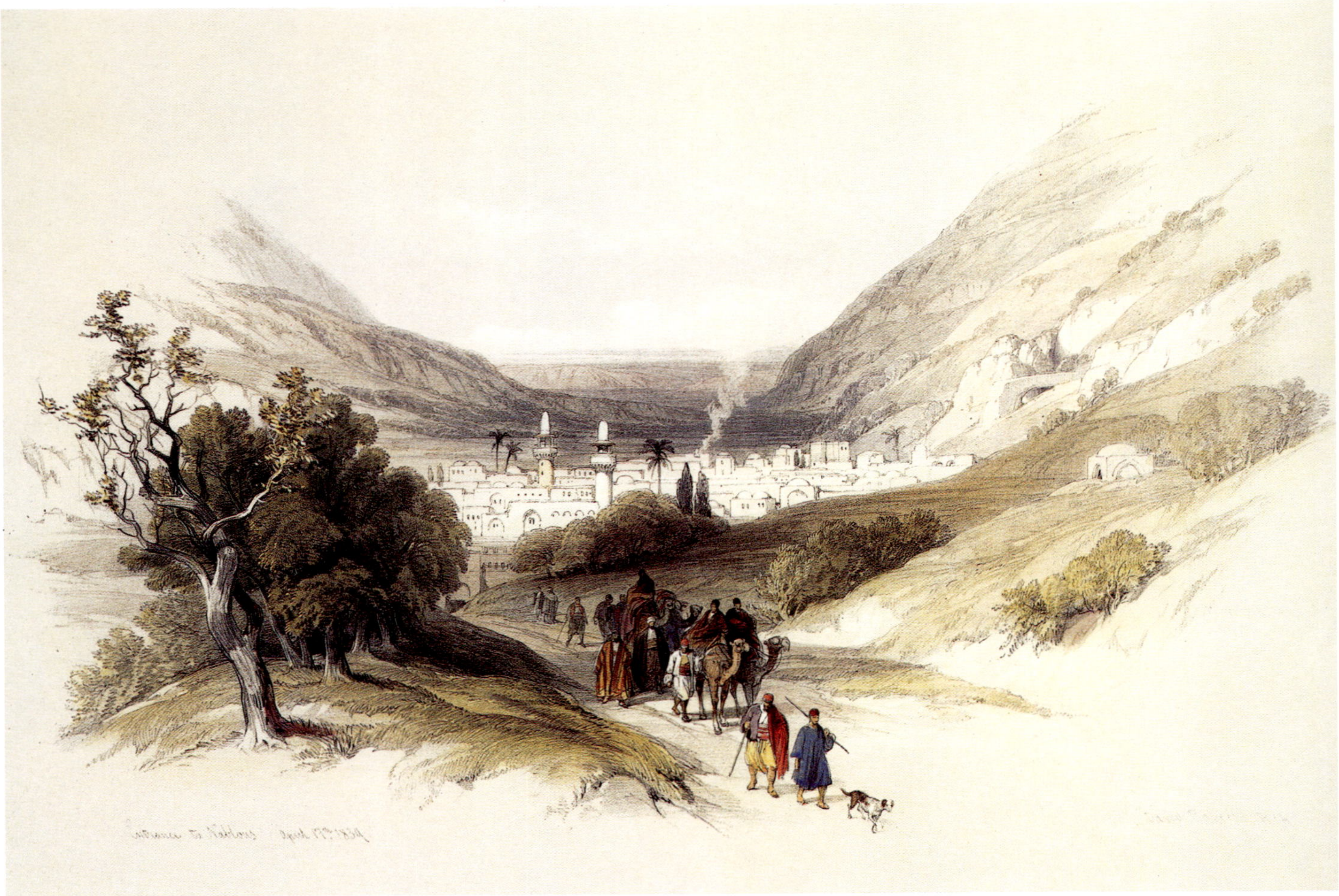

Entrance to Nablous

And Abram passed through the land unto the place of Sichem, unto the plain of Moreh. And the Canaanite [was] then in the land (Gen. 12:6). The Shechem of the Old Testament was a city of very high antiquity and eminent renown. Few in the Holy Land are so beautifully situated. It lies in a narrow valley between Mount Ebal on the north and Mount Gerizim on the south. Roberts says that as he and his companion approached it, **"a scene of luxuriant and almost unparalleled verdure burst upon our view. The whole valley was filled with gardens of vegetables, and orchards of all kinds of fruits, watered by several fountains; we saw nothing to compare with it in all Palestine."**

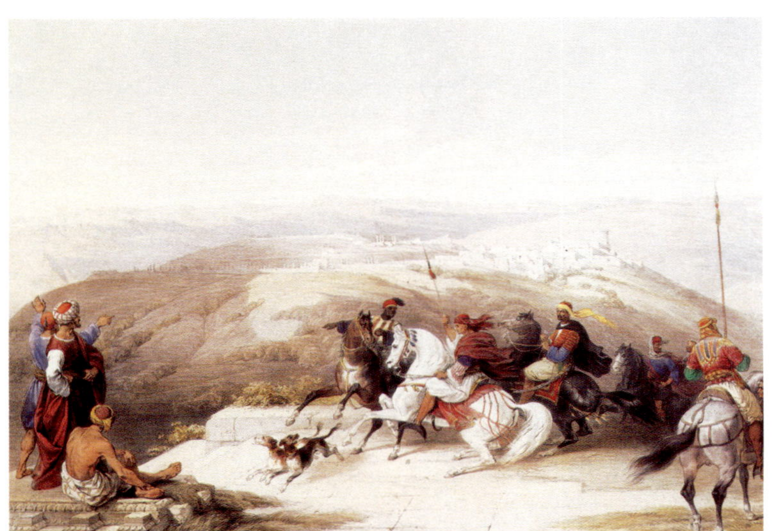

Sebaste - Ancient Samaria

And he bought the hill Samaria of Shemer for two talents of silver, and built on the hill, and called the name of the city which he built, after the name of Shemer, owner of the hill, Samaria (1 Kings 16:24). Sebaste was founded by Omri, King of Israel, about the year 925 B.C. Samaria continued during the centuries to be the chief city of the ten tribes, and during the whole period it was the seat of idolatry. The vast ruins which now exist at Sebaste are chiefly those of the palace of Herod . . . who enriched Samaria with splendid edifices. . . . Such appears to have been the Samaria of the New Testament, in which Philip preached the gospel and where a church was formed by the Apostles.

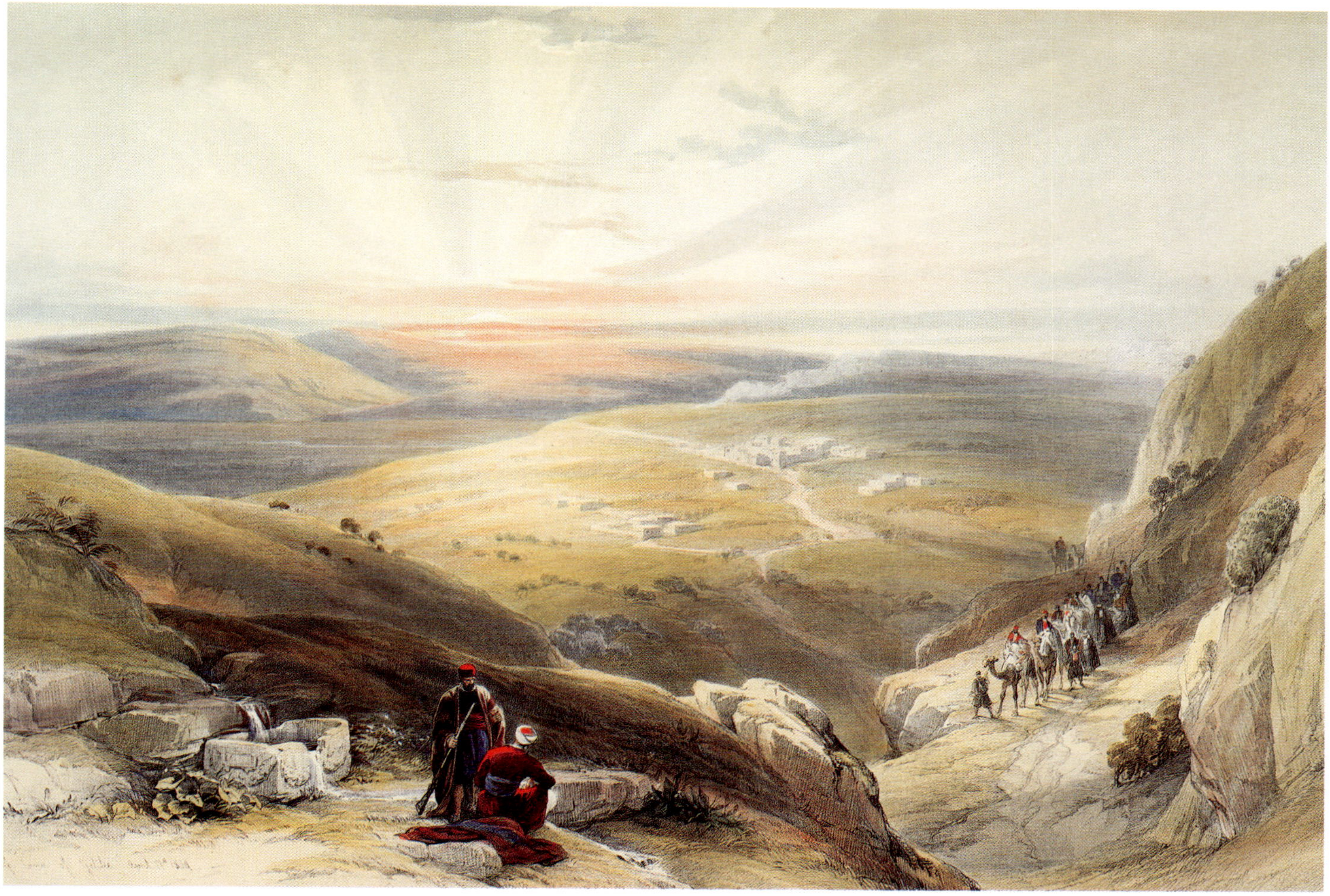

Cana of Galilee

This beginning of miracles did Jesus in Cana of Galilee, and manifested forth his glory; and his disciples believed on him (John 2:11).

The view is full of traditionary holiness. In the small Greek church at the foot of the hill, is shewn by the priest, as an invaluable relic (on the authority of tradition) "one of the water pots" in which the water was changed into wine. For preservation it is built into the wall. The church itself is pronounced to have been raised on the spot where the marriage feast was celebrated.

Mount Tabor
(from the Plain of Estraelon)

And Deborah said unto Barak, Up; for this [is] the day in which the Lord hath delivered Sisera into thine hand: is not the Lord gone out before thee? So Barak went down from Mount Tabor, and ten thousand men after him (Judg. 4:14).

Tabor is a beautiful mountain, wholly of limestone, and rising about a thousand feet above the great Plain of Estraelon. **"The present view,"** observes the artist, **"was taken while crossing the plain, on the road from Jenin to Nazareth."** The figures in the foreground are a caravan of Christian pilgrims whom the artist found resting during the mid-day on their return from Damascus to Jerusalem.

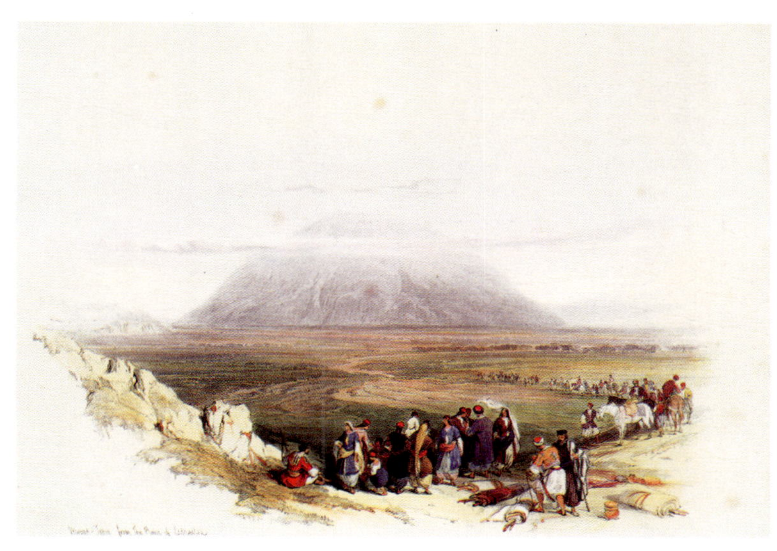

Nazareth, Convent of the Terra Sancta

*And he came and dwelt in a city called Nazareth: that it might be fulfilled which was spoken by the prophets,
He shall be called a Nazarene* (Matt. 2:23).

The site of Nazareth is admirable: and in the days when the land was fully peopled . . . the valley of Nazareth may have been one of the loveliest spots in Palestine. Roberts describes it, **"as if fifteen mountains met to form an enclosure for this delightful spot: . . . a rich and beautiful field in the midst of barren hills; it abounds in fig trees, small gardens and hedges of the prickly pear."** The village stands on the slope of the west side of the valley, the convent at the east end on high ground. In the village there is but one mosque, which, however, forms a prominent feature in the view.

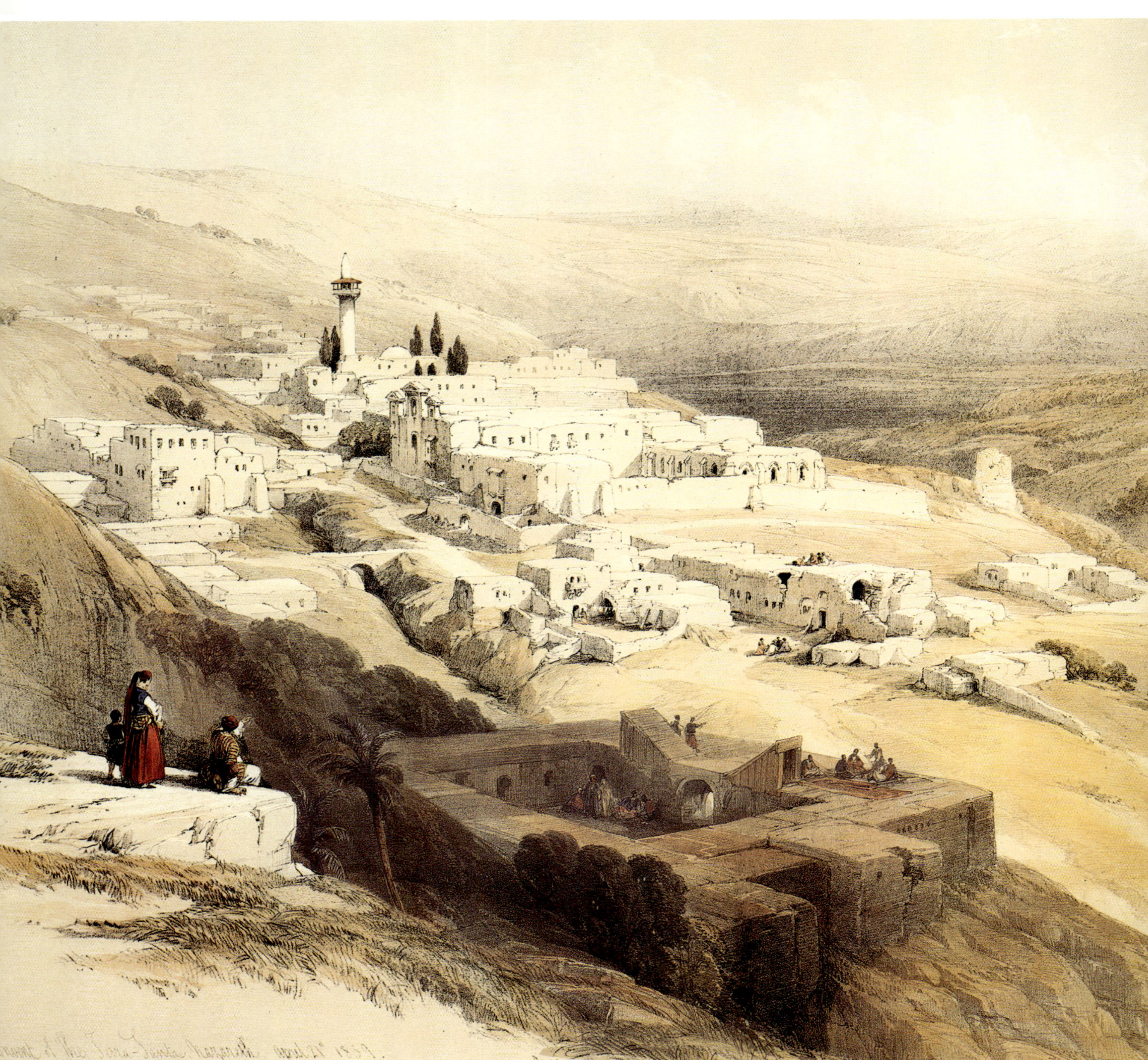

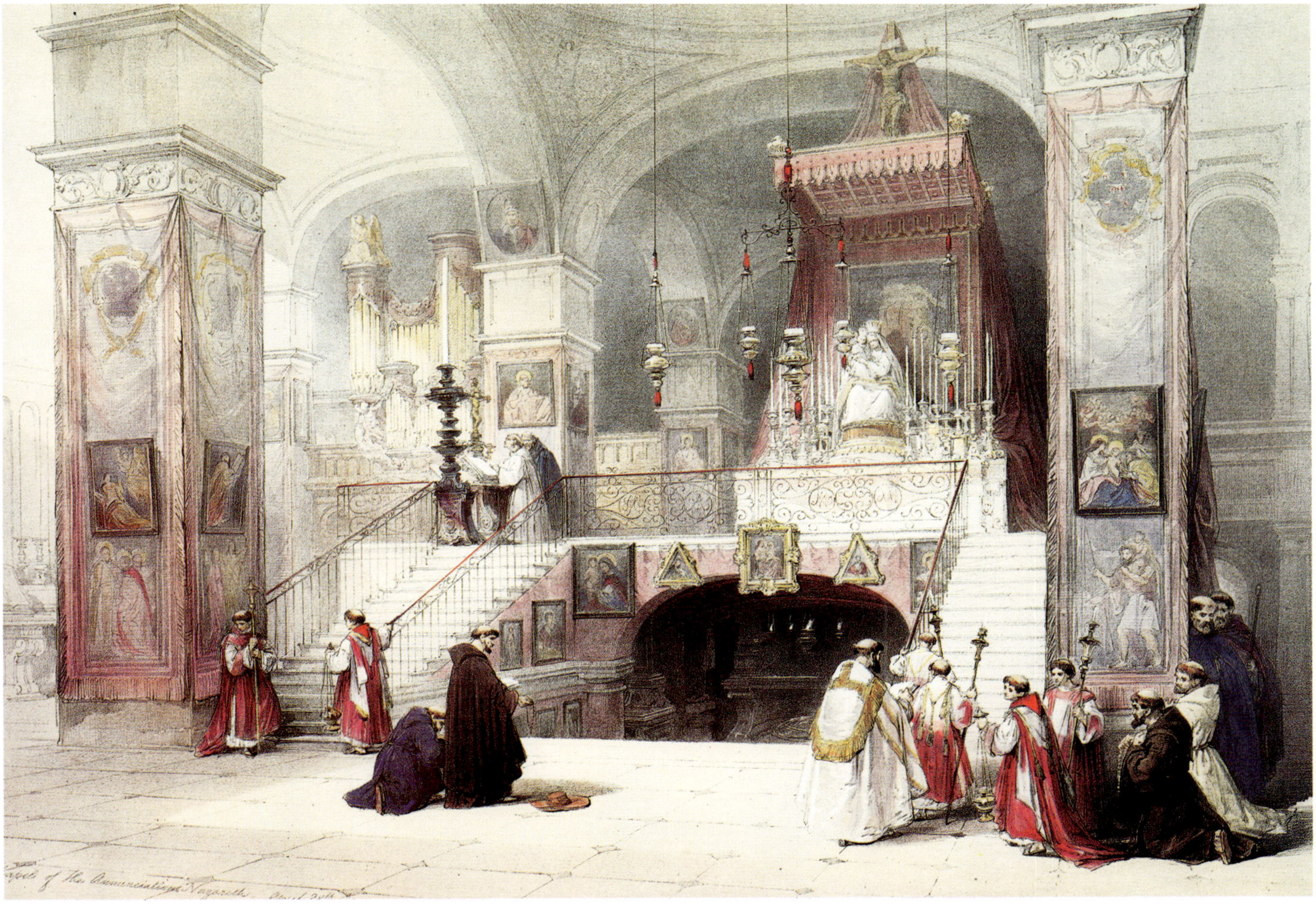

Nazareth, the Church of the Annunciation

The church is a lofty nave, with three elevations. The columns and whole interior of the building are hung with damasked striped silk, which gives it a glowing appearance. **"Finding the door of the church open we went in; it was the hour of vespers, and the chanting of the monks, sustained by the mellow tones of the organ, which came upon us unexpectedly, was solemn and affecting. The interior is small and plain, with massive arches, the hangings of the walls produced a rich effect, the whole impression transported me back to Italy."**

Nazareth, Fountain of the Virgin

And in the sixth month the angel Gabriel was sent from God unto a city of Galilee, named Nazareth, To a virgin espoused to a man whose name was Joseph, of the house of David; and the virgin's name [was] Mary (Luke 1:26).

As this is the only fountain in Nazareth, it is held in great respect by the Christians, not merely as important to the supply of water to the town, but in the belief that to this fountain the mother of our Lord must constantly have come. The church is built over the source; at the spot where, the Greeks say, the virgin was saluted by the angel Gabriel.

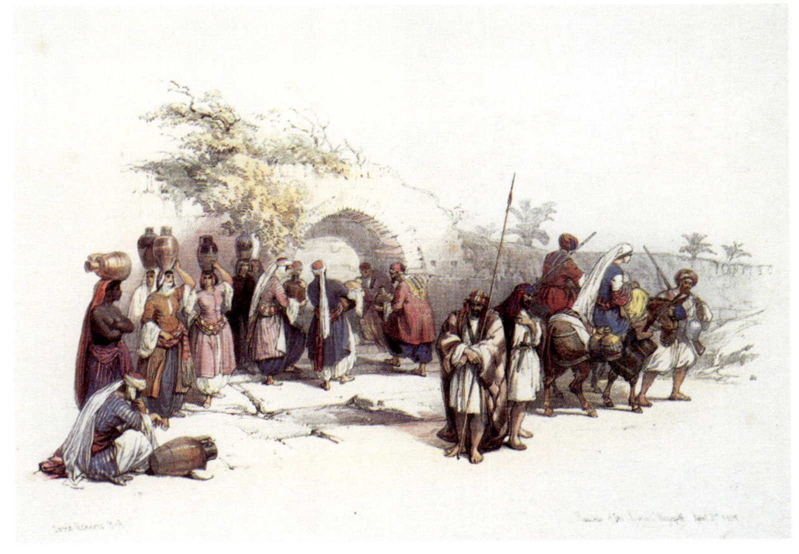

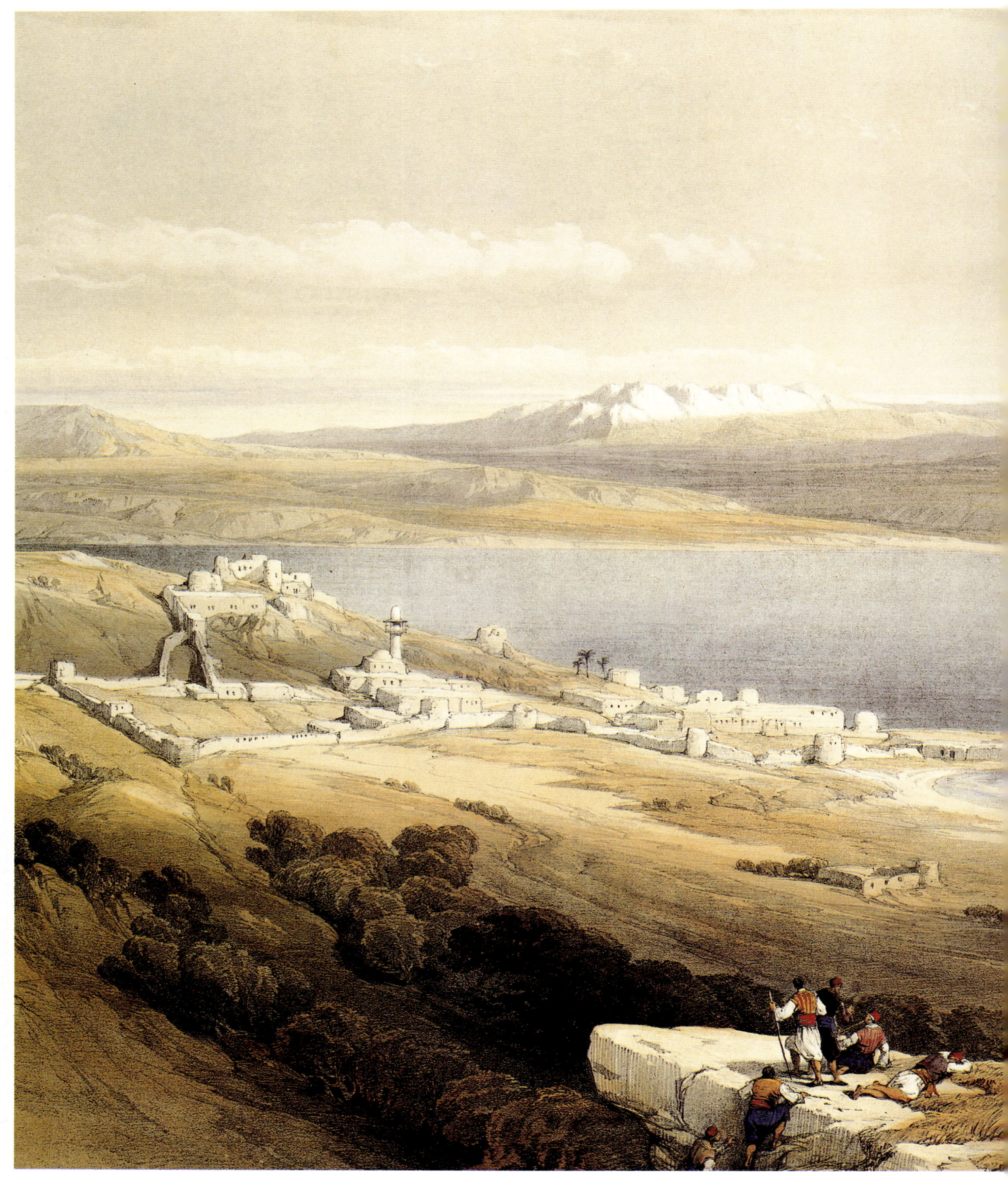

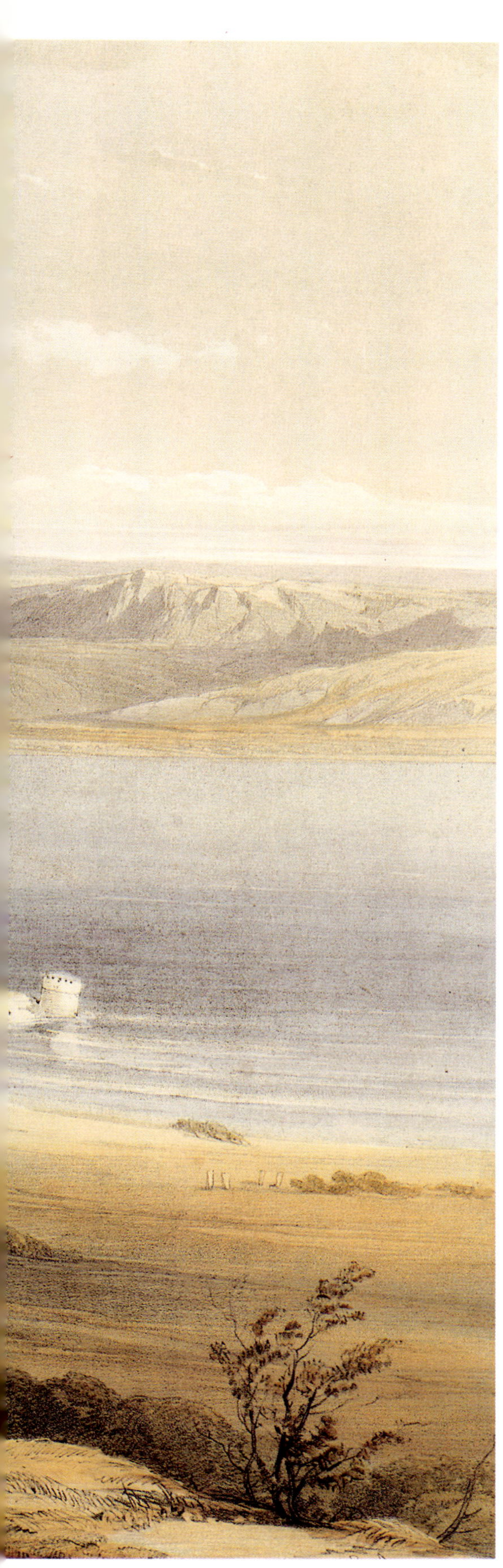

Tiberias on the Sea of Galilee
(looking towards Hermon)

The day following, when the people which stood on the other side of the sea saw that there was none other boat there, save that one whereinto his disciples were entered, and that Jesus went not with his disciples into the boat, but [that] his disciples were gone away alone; (Howbeit there came other boats from Tiberias nigh unto the place where they did eat bread, after that the Lord had given thanks:) When the people therefore saw that Jesus was not there, neither his disciples, they also took shipping, and came to Capernaum, seeking for Jesus (John 6:22-24).

The ancient city of Tiberias, built by Herod Antipas, has long since perished. Herod compelled a population from the surrounding provinces to fill his city, adorned it with structures, of which the very fragments are stately: gave it peculiar priveleges; and building a palace, which was one of the wonders of the land, declared Tiberias the capital of Galilee. The ruins in the sketch are those of the modern city prostrated by the earthquake. The view commands various sites memorable from their connexion with the Scriptures . . . in the horizon is the majestic Hermon, 10,000 feet above the Mediterranean.

Tiberias
(from the Walls)

This sketch, in addition to the view of the city, gives in the distance, crowning a lofty hill, the city of Safed. The land is peculiarly liable to earthquakes. Safed was fearfully visited in the middle of the last century (1759): but a still heavier visitation befell it in 1837. Safed is venerated as one of the four holy cities of Judea, the others being Jerusalem, Hebron, and Tiberias.

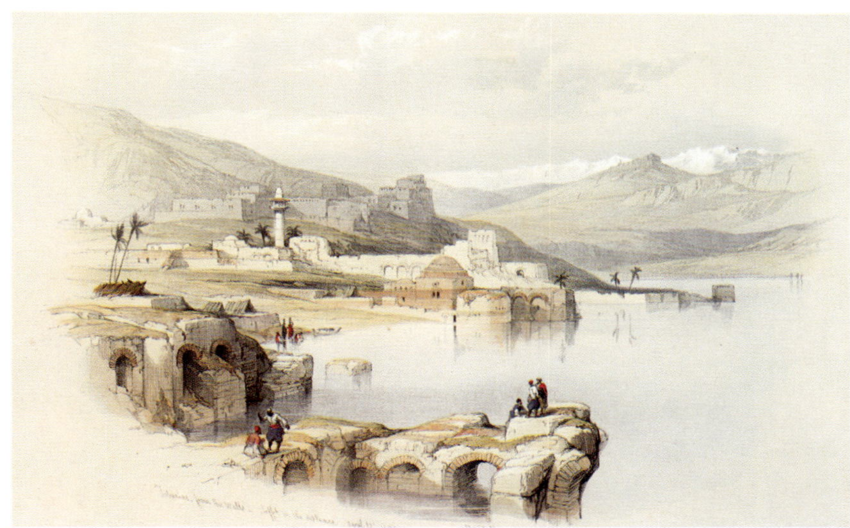

Cape Blanco (Rosh Hanikra)

This promontory forms one of the most striking natural objects on the coast of Syria. At the foot of Cape Blanco – also called by the natives Ras-el-Abiad (the white promontory), from its bleached front – the road ascends, and winds along the face of the cliff to a startling elevation.

Ancient Jaffa, Looking South

And [as for] the western border, ye shall even have the great sea for a border: this shall be your west border (Num. 34:6).

Jaffa . . . rose into early importance as the chief harbor of Judaea. Like all eastern cities the interior disappoints the eye. Narrow streets loaded with mire in winter and choked with dust in the summer, a struggling population compressed into hovels which seem the natural nests of disease. . . . A Greek, a Latin, and an Armenian Convent constitute the town and its people. It was the nearest port to the Holy City. The figures in the forground are Polish Jews returning home from their pilgrimage to Jerusalem.

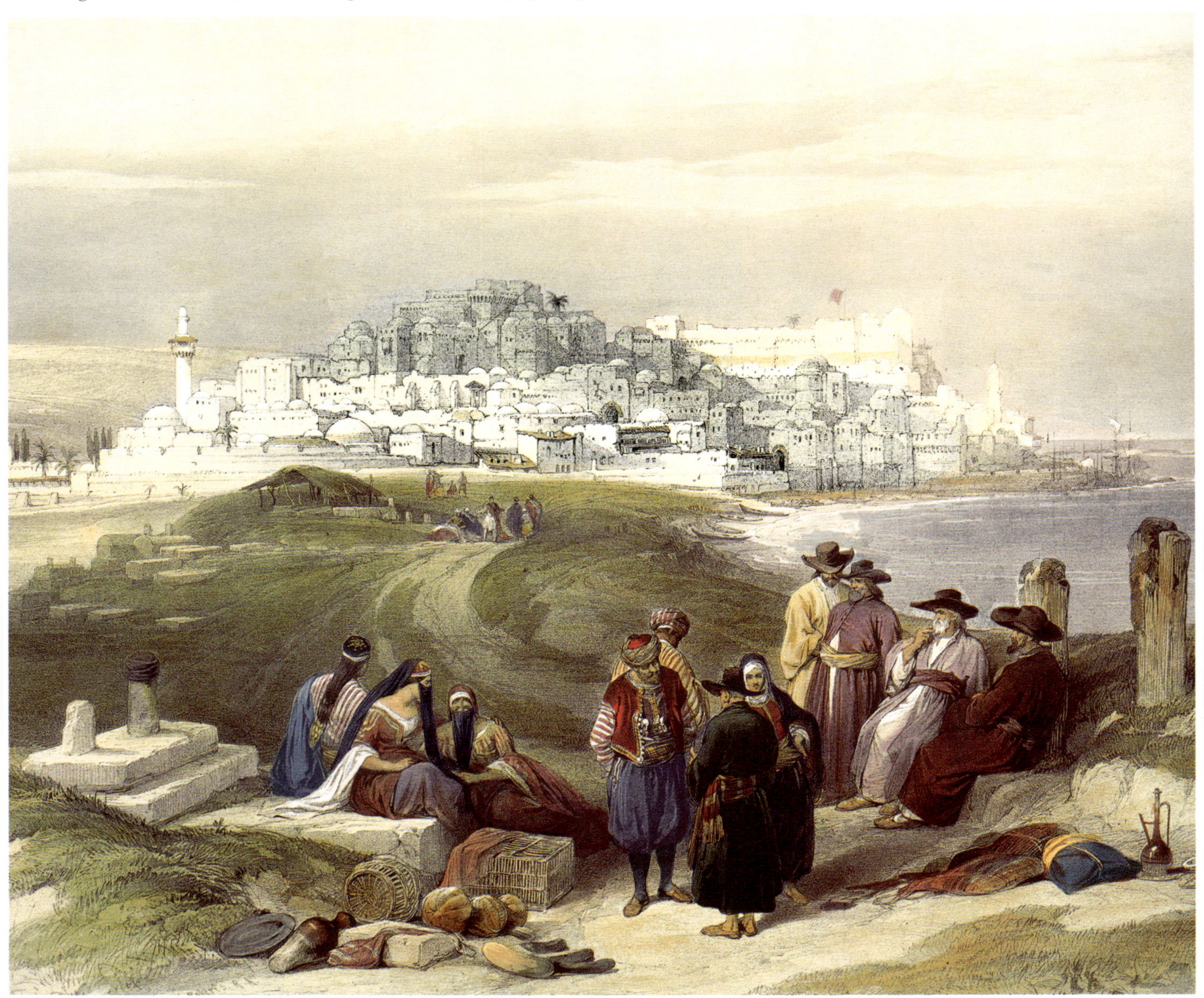

(St. Jean d'Acre) Acre *(below)*

Neither did Asher drive out the inhabitants of Accho, nor the inhabitants of Zidon, nor of Ahlab, nor of Achzib, nor of Helbah, nor of Aphik, nor of Rehob: But the Asherites dwelt among the Canaanites, the inhabitants of the land: for they did not drive them out (Judg. 1:31-32).

"This view gives the sea face of Acre, exhibiting a striking succession of domes, minarets, and that general style of ornamental building which is so attractive to the eye at a distance, but which so frequently disappoints it on a nearer view. Still the oriental architecture has a charm of its own . . . combining all that was romantic in the East, with all that was superb."

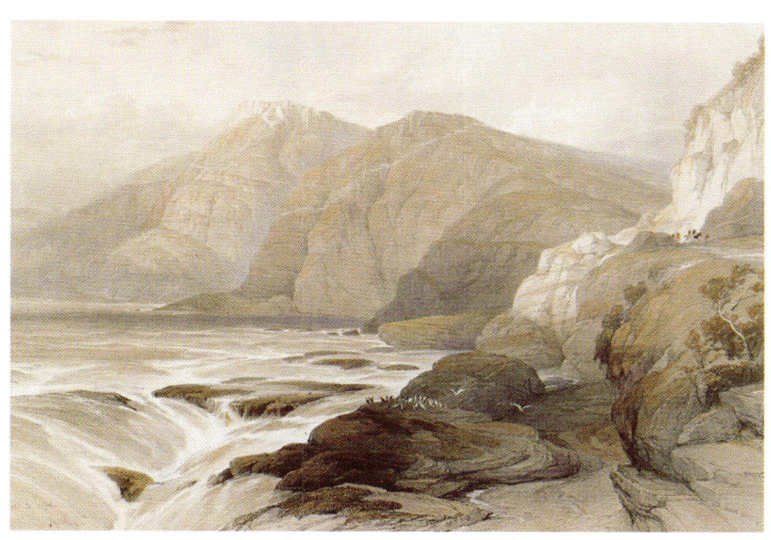

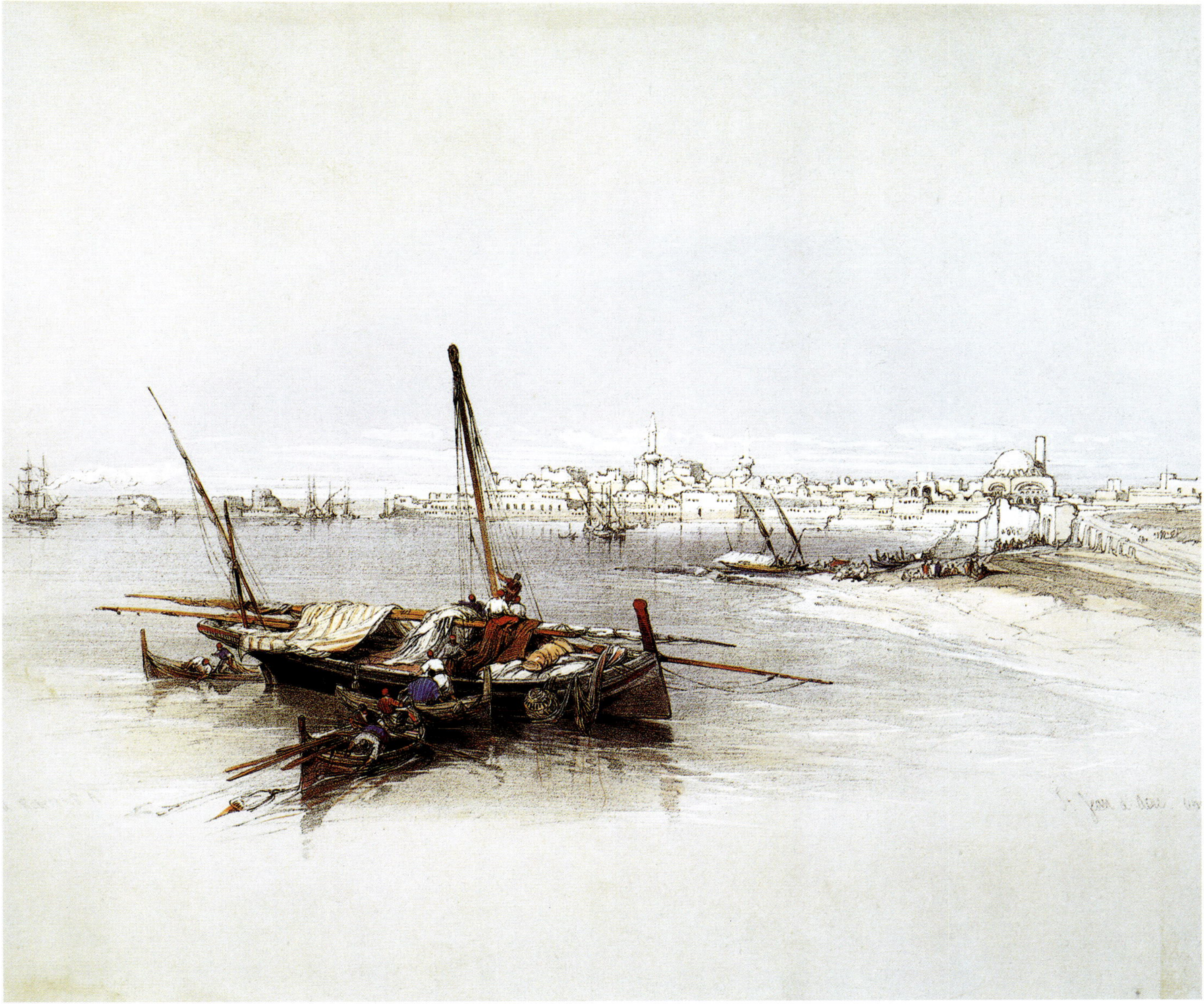

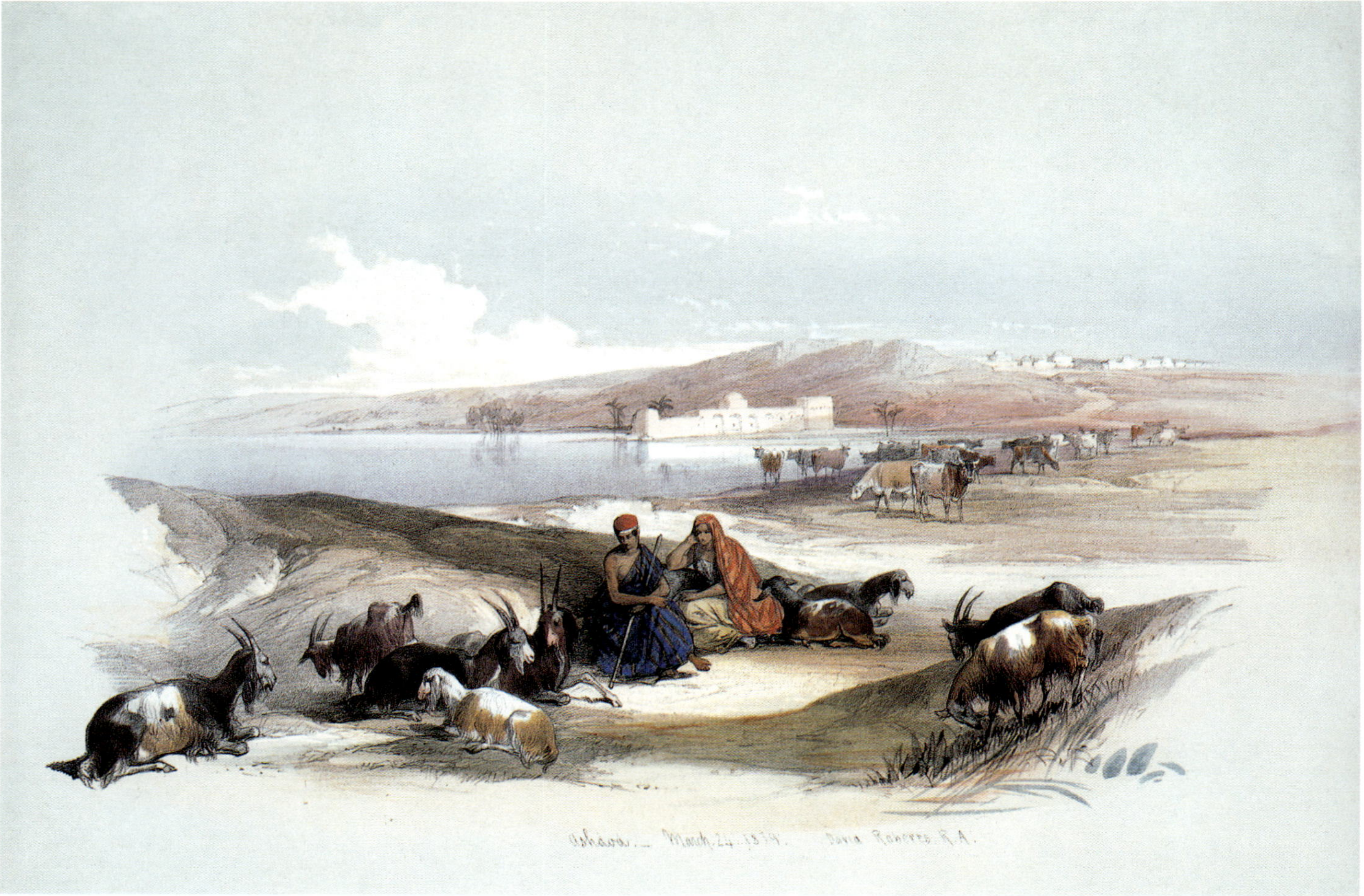

Ancient Ashdod

In the year that Tartan came unto Ashdod, (when Sargon the king of Assyria sent him,) and fought against Ashdod, and took it (Isa. 20:1). **"Ashdod of the Old Testament, Azotus of the New, and Ashdod of the present day, stands about ten miles from Jaffa. It is now but a wretched village, though its position in the midst of a fertile country, and commanding a portion of the route along the coast, may yet restore it to some share of its early importance."** In the Jewish annals it is distinguished as one of the five chief cities of the Philistines. Ashdod was the city to which the captive ark was brought after the defeat of the Israelite army.

Haifa, Mt. Carmel
(Caiphas, Looking toward Mt. Carmel)

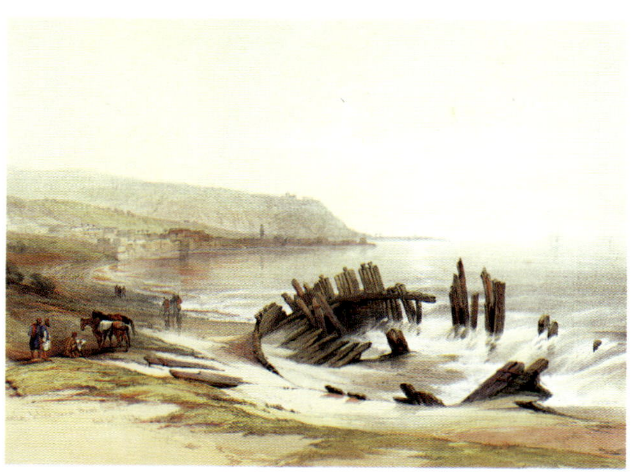

Now therefore send, [and] gather to me all Israel unto mount Carmel. . . . And Elijah came unto all the people, and said, How long halt ye between two opinions? if the Lord [be] God, follow him: but if Baal, [then] follow him. And the people answered him not a word (1 Kings 18:19 - 21).

"This view is taken from near the mouth of the River Kishon, and in the foreground characteristically lies one of the wrecks which constantly strew this exposed shore. . . . On the left is seen the summit of Mt. Tabor, with portions of the Lesser Hermon and Gilboa, and the opposite Mountain of Samaria. The eye then rests on the long line of Carmel, with the 'Convent of Elias' on its summit, and the town of Caipha glittering at its foot. A succession of mountain ridges stretch from East to West: and to the right is a 'sea of hills,' surmounted by Hermon, with its icy crown."

Askelon

And the Spirit of the LORD came upon him, and he went down to Ashkelon, and slew thirty men of them, and took their spoil, and gave change of garments unto them which expounded the riddle. And his anger was kindled, and he went up to his father's house (Judges 14:19).

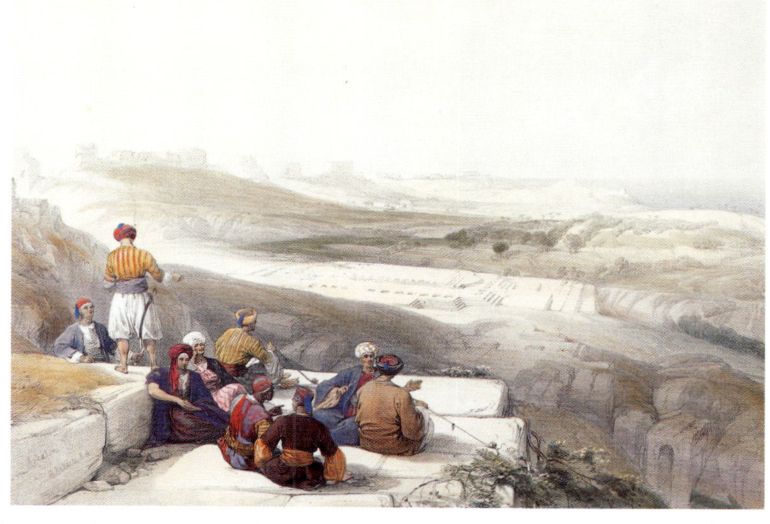

Askelon, known in early Jewish history as one of the chief cities of the Philistines, flourished until the great fall of the Jewish cities. It was once a place of opulent trade, yet it never had a port, or its only port was artificial, and formed by the mole. The shore seems once to have been covered with stately buildings, from the granite pillars and blocks of stone, and it is to Ibrahim Pasha that we owe the chief indulgence which Askelon now offers to European curiosity. He ordered the ground to be extensively cleared, and the result was the discovery of several magnificent ruins, and among the rest the ground plan of a temple, of which some columns remain. Another discovery was the site of a Christian church, of which the pavement and the bases of the columns have been preserved.

Gaza

And the border of the Canaanites was from Sidon, as thou comest to Gerar, unto Gaza; as thou goest, unto Sodom, and Gomorrah, and Admah, and Zeboim, even unto Lasha (Gen. 10:19).

Gaza stands on the summit of a hill, half-a-mile from the sea. Its history has been a succession of suffering at the hands of every invader of Palestine. A history of this city would be one of the most striking vicissitude; Gaza was among the earliest cities of Canaan mentioned in the Old Testament. The inhabitants still refer to Samson's carrying away the gates, nay boldly point out he spot which they were taken; and the small domed building on the right in the engraving marks the spot to which he is supposed to have borne them.

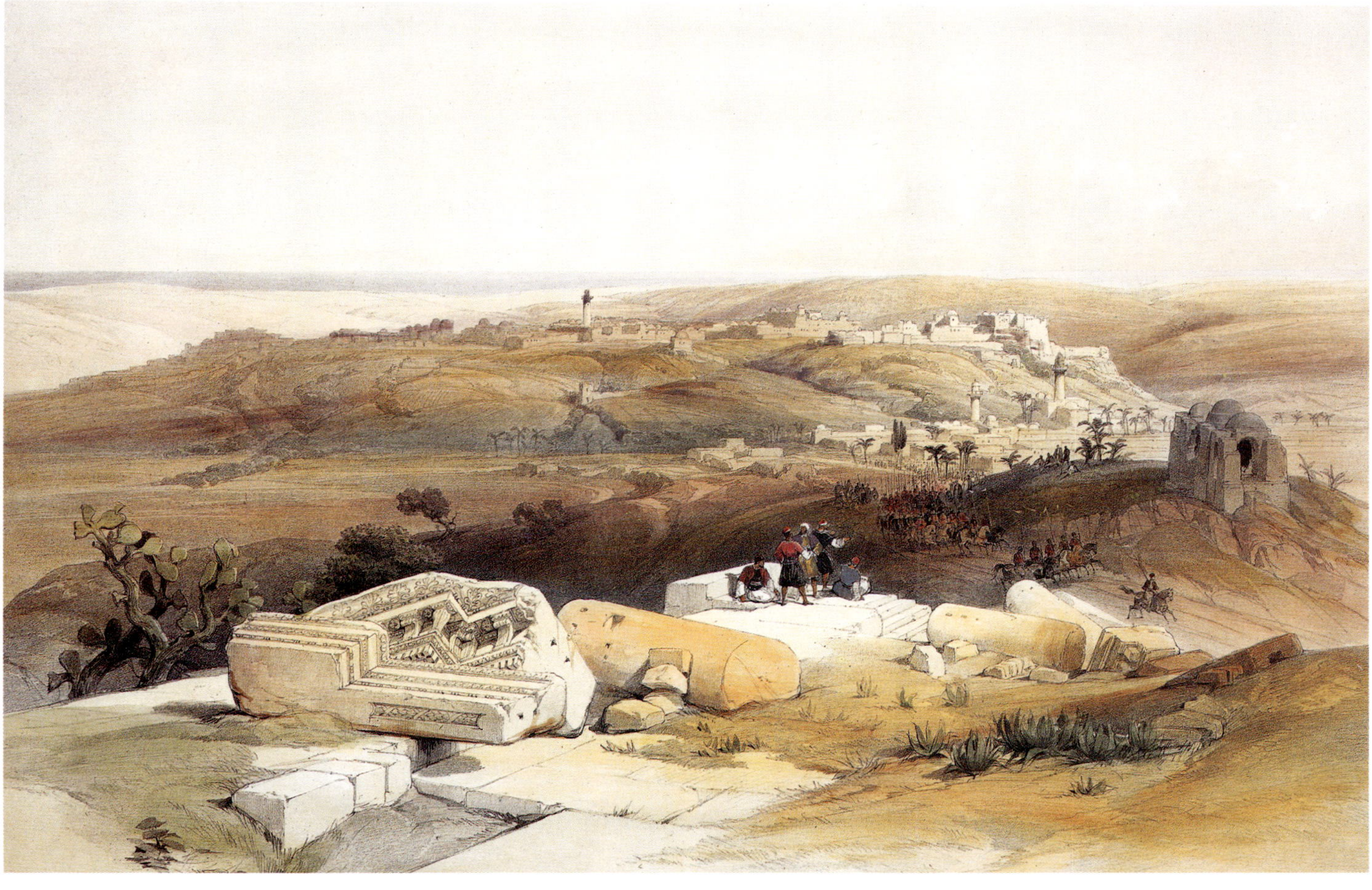

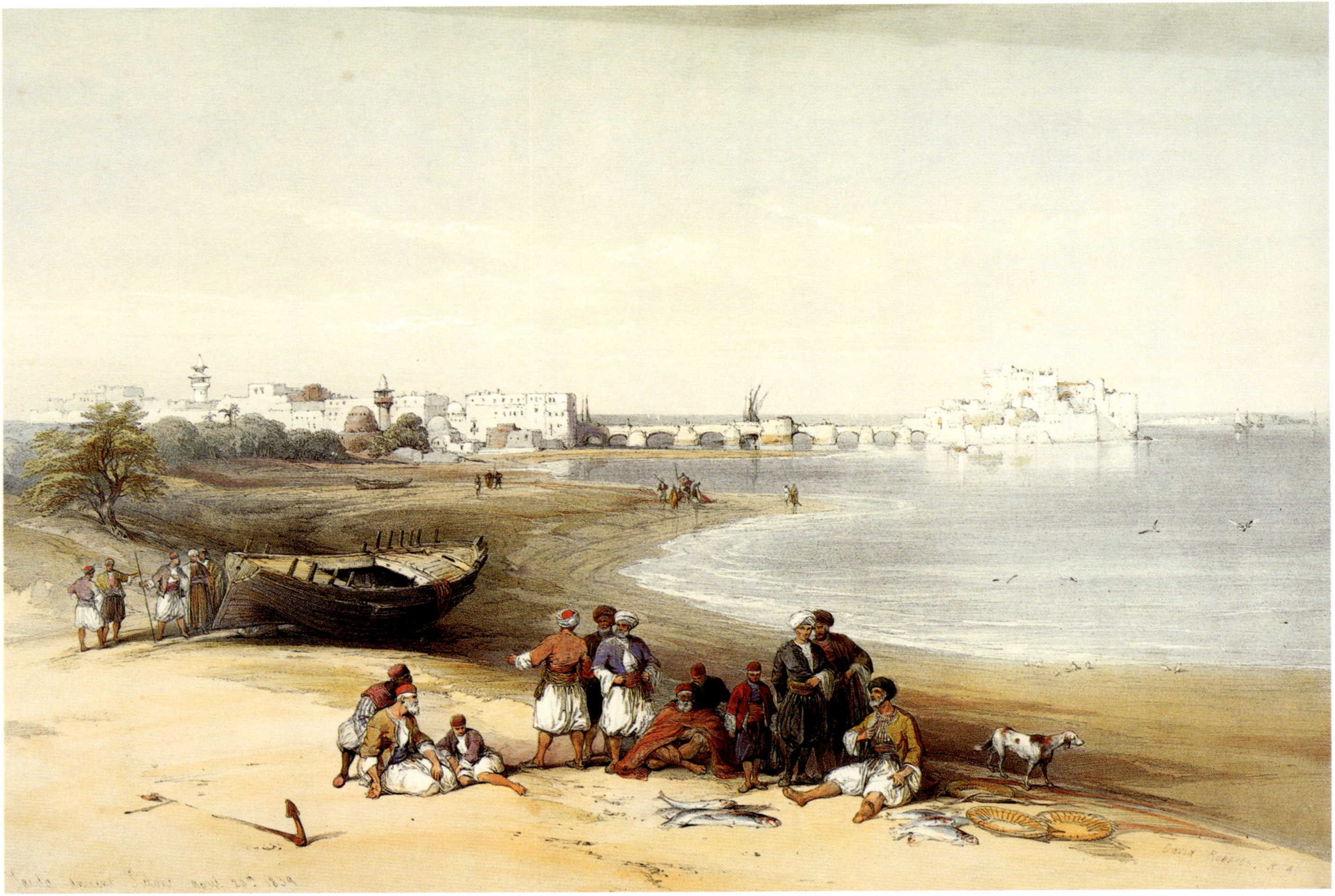

Sidon

But Jesus withdrew himself with his disciples to the sea: and a great multitude from Galilee followed him, and from Judaea, And from Jerusalem, and from Idumaea, and [from] beyond Jordan; and they about Tyre and Sidon, a great multitude, when they had heard what great things he did, came unto him (Mark 3:7-8).

Sidon, a name familiar to all the readers of ancient history, and renewed in our recollections by the brilliant Syrian campaign of 1841, is one of the oldest cities in the world; and has been distinguished for its commerce, its opulence, and its vicissitudes, from almost the earliest period of its existence. Christianity took root there so early as the first preaching of the Apostles; and Paul, on his way to Rome, found converts, and apparently a church.

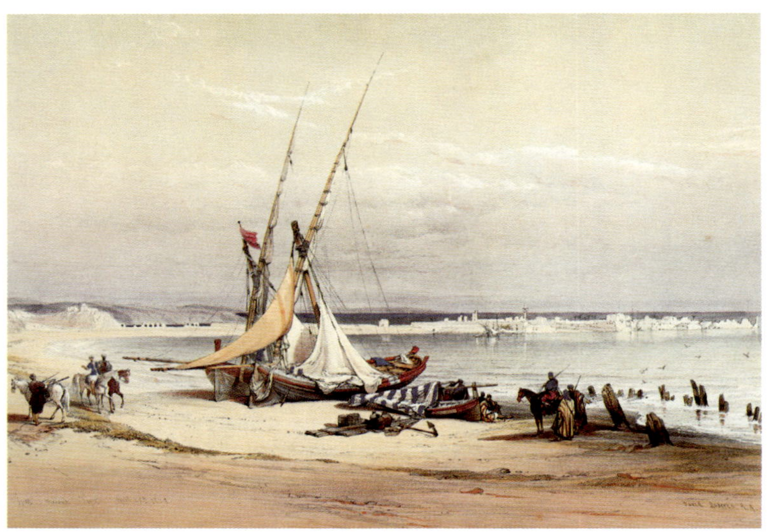

General View of Tyre

Therefore thus saith the Lord God; Behold, I [am] against thee, O Tyrus, and will cause many nations to come up against thee, as the sea causeth his waves to come up. And they shall destroy the walls of Tyrus, and break down her towers: I will also scrape her dust from her, and make her like the top of a rock (Ezek. 26:3-4).

This scene comprehends the sites of two of the most memorable cities of antiquity — the Tyre of the mainland, and the Tyre of the island, with the causeway connecting them. At the time of the sketch, some vessels were lying in the bay; few, but sufficient to carry on the traffic of this once queen of the commercial world. This once renowned city is now but a diminutive town, carrying on a struggling commerce in the tobacco of the neighboring hills, with some wood and charcoal from the more distant mountains.

Baalbec, Remains of the Western Portico

So Joshua took all that land, the hills, and all the south country, and all the land of Goshen, and the valley, and the plain, and the mountain of Israel, and the valley of the same; [Even] from the mount Halak, that goeth up to Seir, even unto Baalgad in the valley of Lebanon under mount Hermon: and all their kings he took, and smote them, and slew them. Joshua made war a long time with all those kings (Josh. 11:16-18).

The enormous size of the marble blocks of which the columns are composed is distinctly shown here. The intricate pattern and rich sculpture of this portion cannot be looked on without the highest admiration at the fancy and skill of Roman workmanship. A late traveller thus touchingly conveys his impression of this noble and solemn scene: **"The sun was fast sinking behind Lebanon, and the shadows of the mountain were gradually encroaching on the silent and desert plain. I directed my steps to the more perfect Temple, standing in the area below, but the masses of prostrate columns and fractured marbles seem to interdict an approach."**

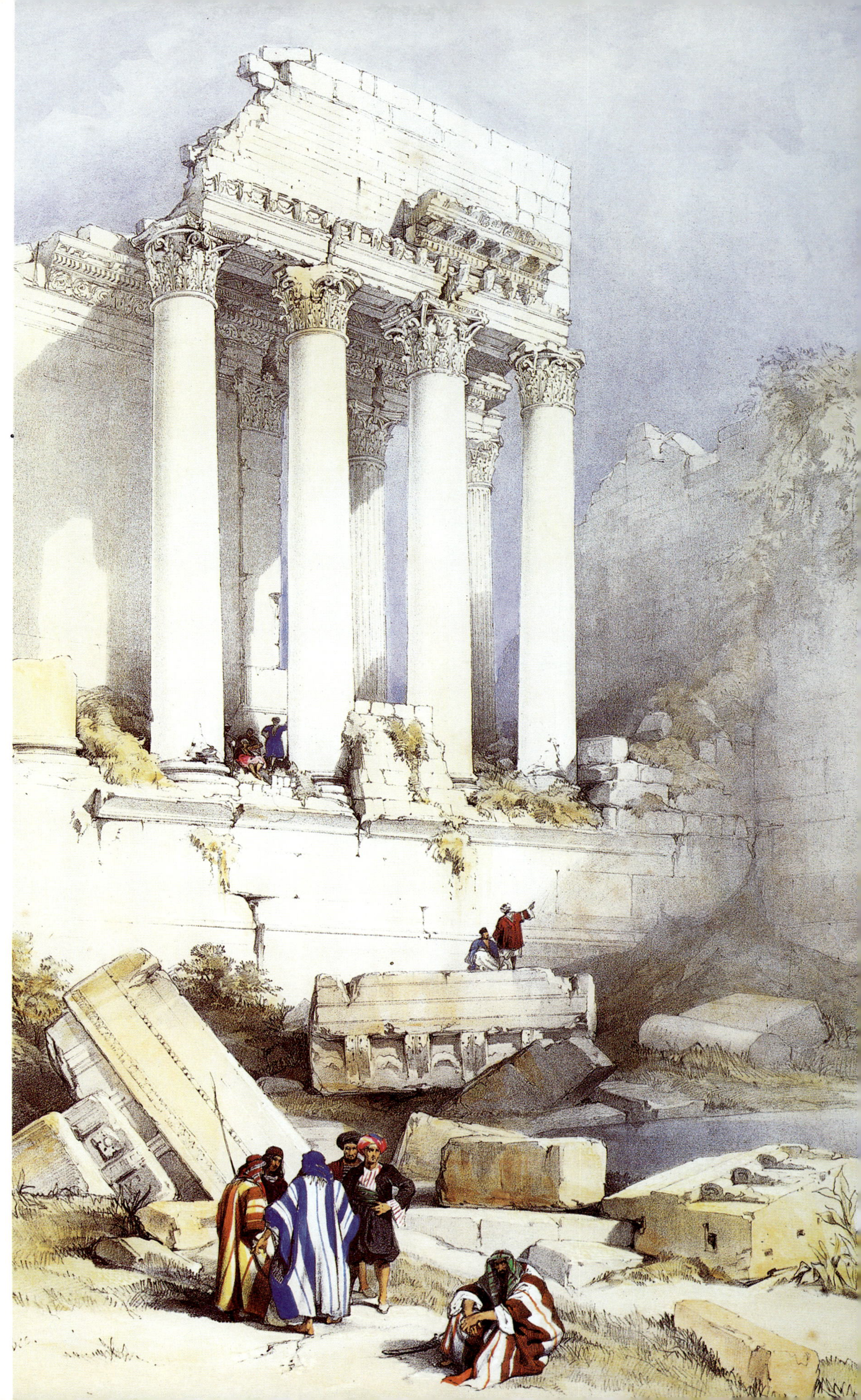

Petra, the Eastern End of the Valley

Send ye the lamb to the ruler of the land from Sela to the wilderness, unto the mount of the daughter of Zion (Isa. 16:1).

In advancing towards the termination of the valley, two masses of sculpture peculiarly attract the eye. One, the more distant in the present view, resembling the Khasné, but having eight Corinthian pillars. The edifice in front is of larger dimensions, and has four entrances, adorned by pilasters and ornaments in the florid style. Travellers have, in general, pronounced them "either temples or tombs." The opinion now offered is that the majority of those sculptured excavations were for the sole purpose of gratifying the eye; a noble indulgence of the national taste for ornament, a natural and fine employment of the superfluous wealth of an active and opulent people compressed within a boundary, narrow but singularly adapted for the most novel and magnificent decoration.

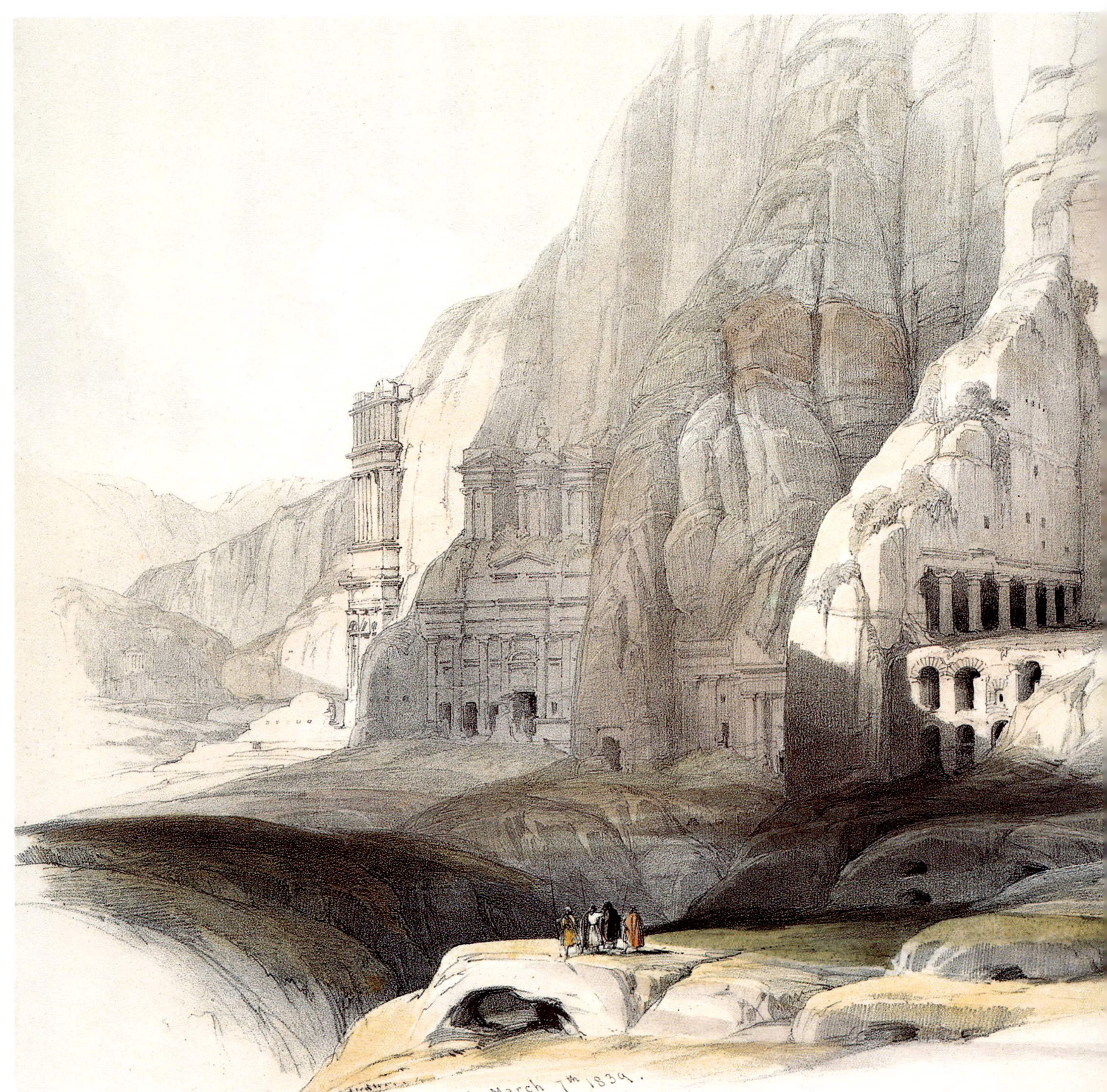

Petra, the Arch Crossing the Ravine

For it shall be, [that], as a wandering bird cast out of the nest, [so] the daughters of Moab shall be at the fords of Arnon (Isa. 16:2).

Near the mouth of the chasm El Sik, an arch, at a considerable height, connects the rocks on either side. Time has destroyed whatever evidence might have existed of its actual purpose, and the question now is whether it was formed for ornament, for defence, or for simple communication. But with that fondness for decoration which seems to have neglected no opportunity of exhibiting itself, the portion below the arch is excavated into niches, which, it may be presumed, contained statues, possibly idols, the protecting deities of this extraordinary city. Some remains of a gateway or barrier built of large square stones show that the security of the entrance was intrusted to more sufficient guardians. Petra, though deserted, is not untrodden; a rude and infrequent traffic passes through it still; and it happened that while the artist was employed on this sketch a caravan from Gaza, consisting of 40 camels on their way to Màan on the Damascus road, passed through the ravine.

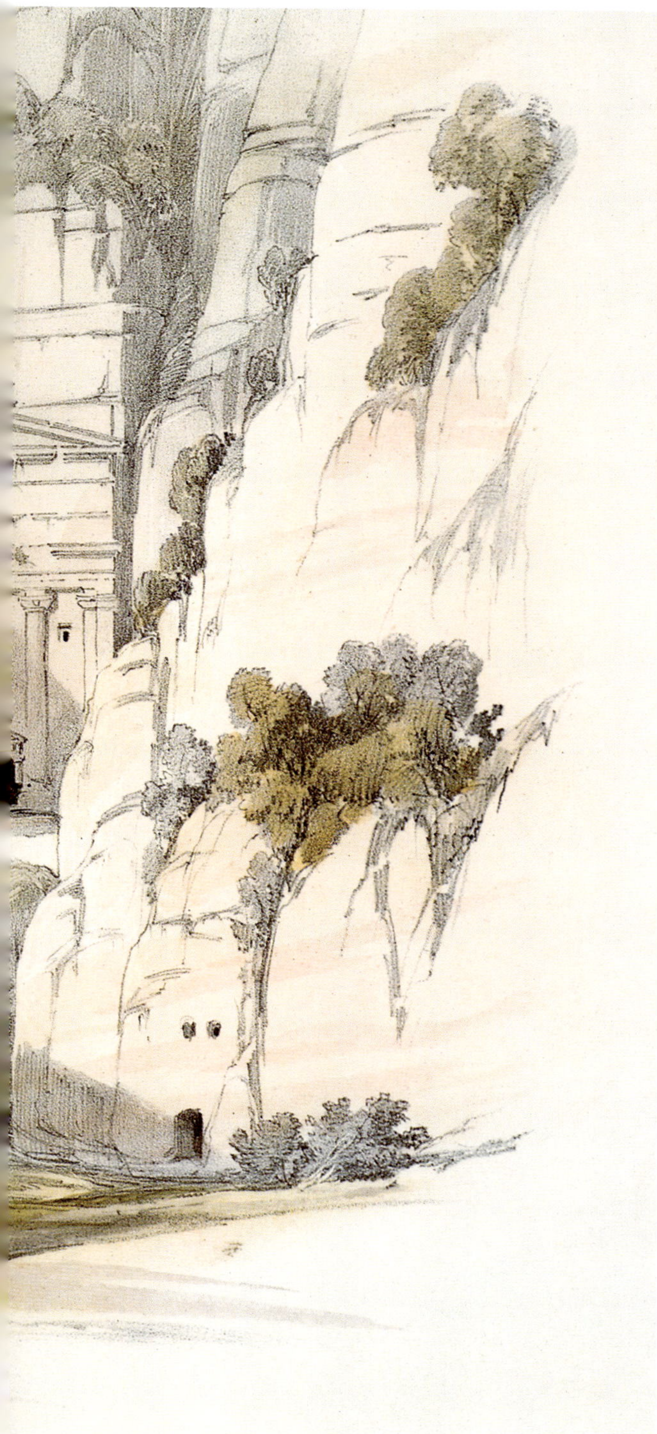

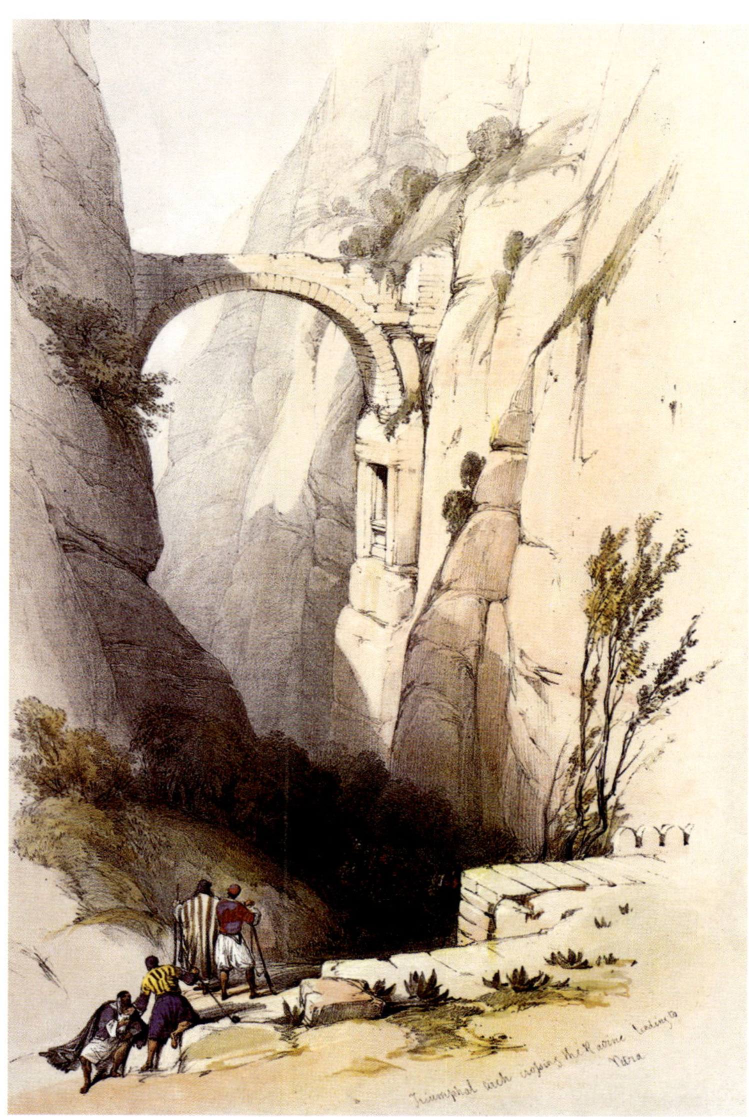

Mt. Sinai
(An Encampment of the Aulad-Sa'id)

And Moses went up unto God, and the Lord called unto him out of the mountain, saying, Thus shalt thou say to the house of Jacob, and tell the children of Israel; Ye have seen what I did unto the Egyptians, and [how] I bare you on eagles' wings, and brought you unto myself. Now therefore, if ye will obey my voice indeed, and keep my covenant, then ye shall be a peculiar treasure unto me above all people: for all the earth [is] mine (Exod. 19:3-5).

"At five o'clock we arrived at the encampment of the Aulad-Sa'id. Our painted pavilion looked a little out of place beside the black Arab tents, which were more in character with the dark and wild mountains which formed the background of the picture, and the wild figures who were moving about. . . . I had never seen a spot more wild and desolate."

Monastery of St. Katherine

This scene represents the arrival of the caravan of the artist and his companions. The mountain is red granite, without a trace of vegetation, and rises majestically to the height of 5,000 feet. The monastery has been built in the form of a square fortress of hewn granite, and flanked with towers . . . its strength forms the chief security of the inhabitants; for it is accessible only by a projecting trap door. The monastery is large and resembles a small town, containing many buildings, several courts and storehouses, a mosque with a minaret, and a chapel.

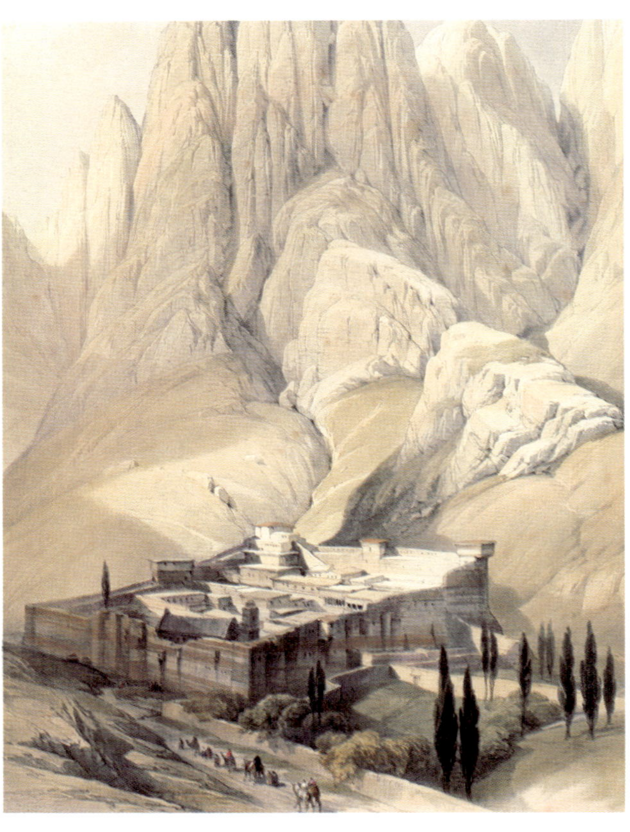

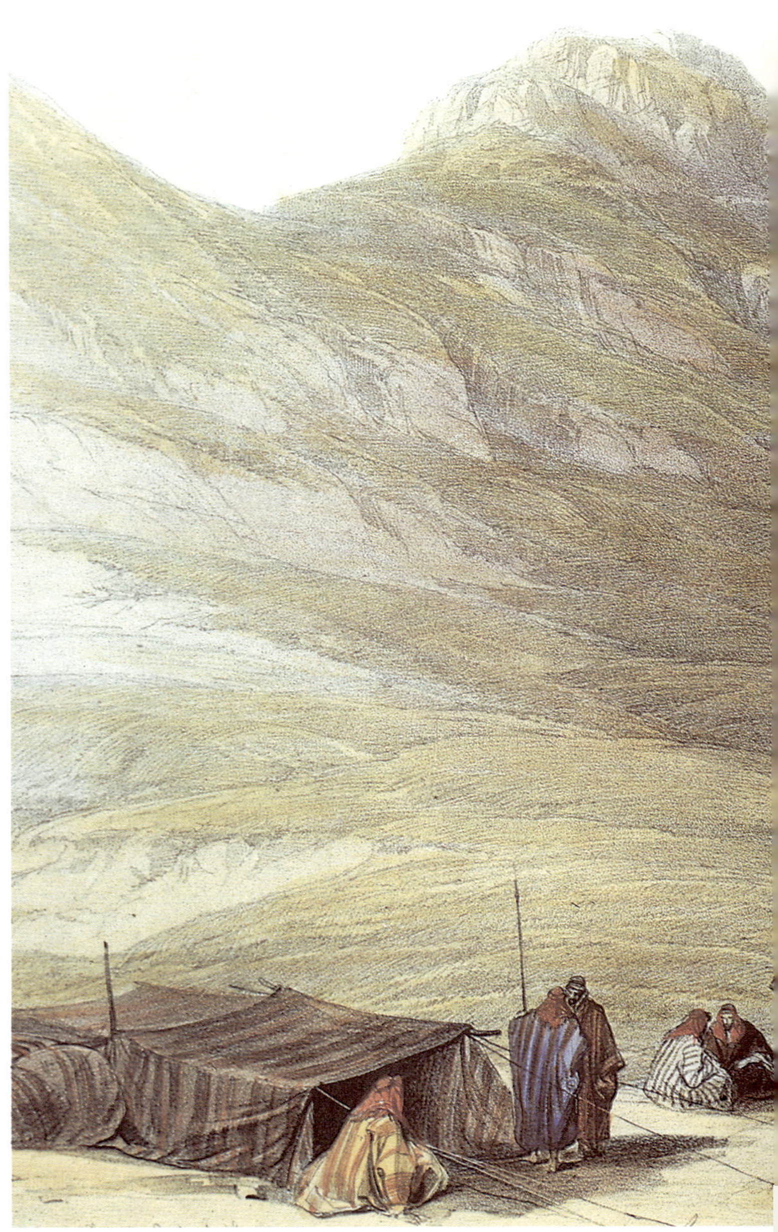

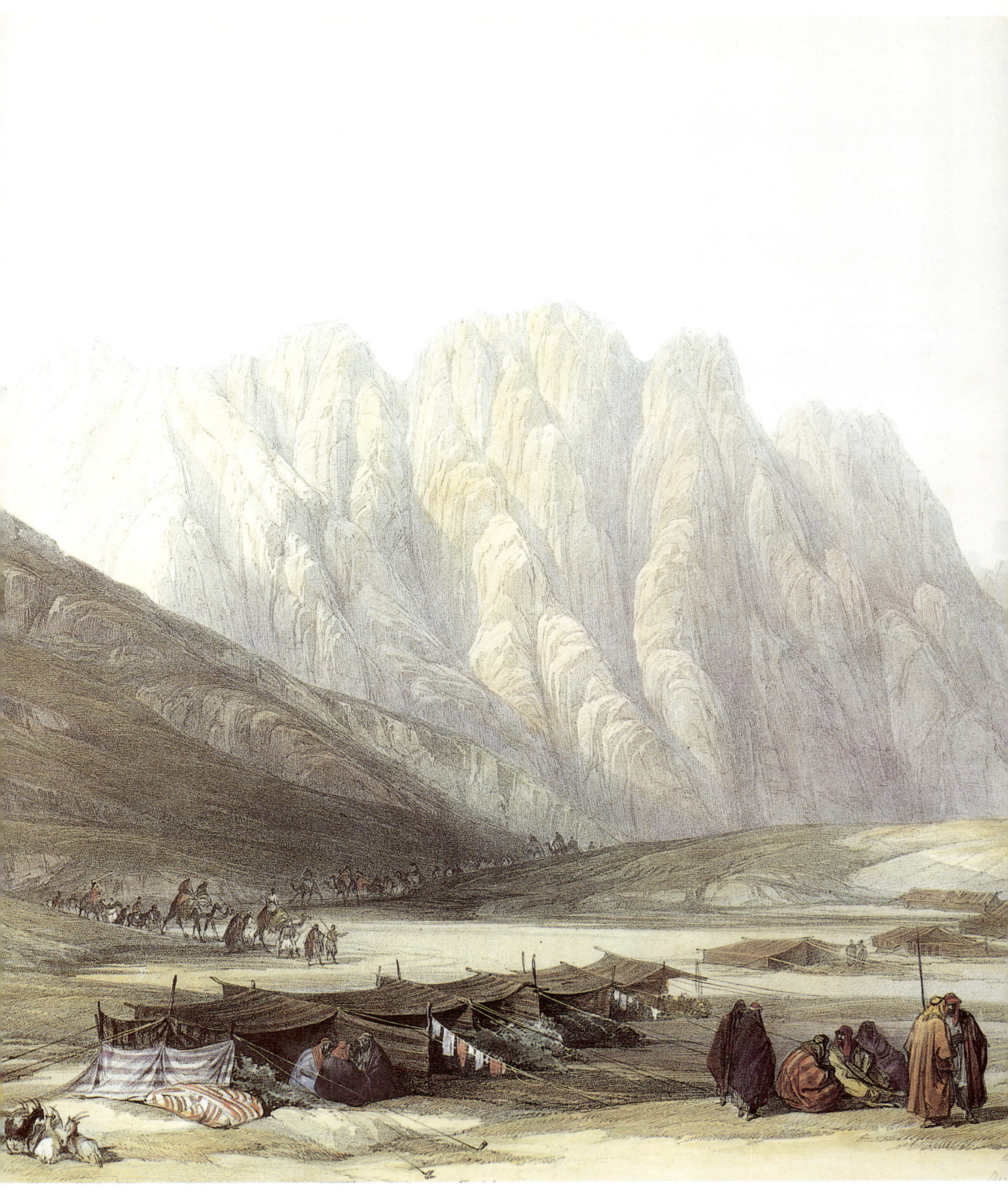

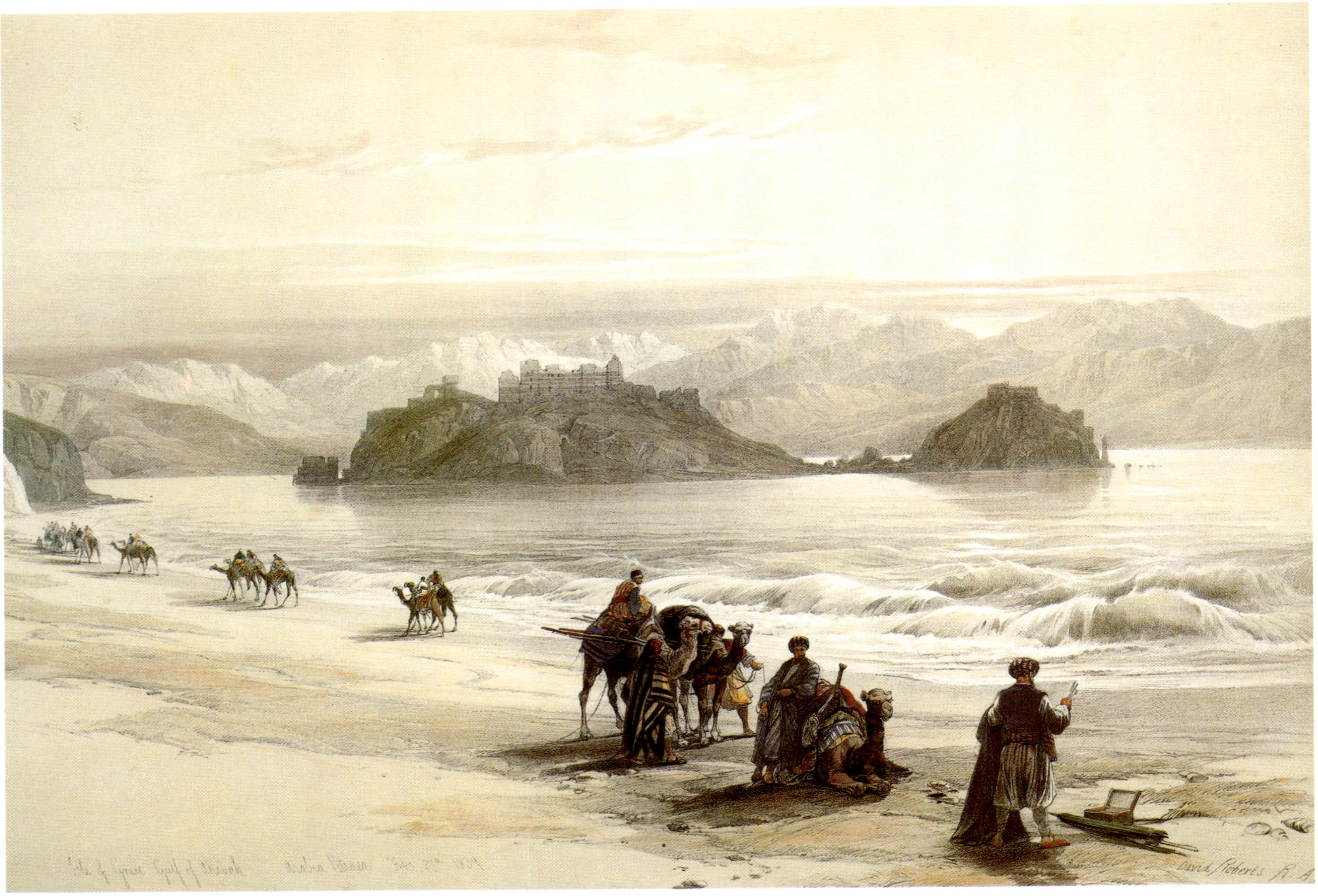

The Coral Island (Island of Graia)

The wild beasts of the desert shall also meet with the wild beasts of the island, and the satyr shall cry to his fellow; the screech owl also shall rest there, and find for herself a place of rest (Isa. 34:14).

Traditionally the Beni-Sa'id Arabs believe that a great city once existed on the island with a magnificent harbor . . . now not a solitary sail is ever seen. The waters teem with fish, but only one man was seen at Akabah pursuing fishing as an employment: he caught a great number of excellent fish and supplied the caravan of the artist's party with a great treat after the fare of the desert. The form of the island and its ruins, backed by the distant range of mountains and the effect under which they are represented, give great beauty to this highly picturesque subject.

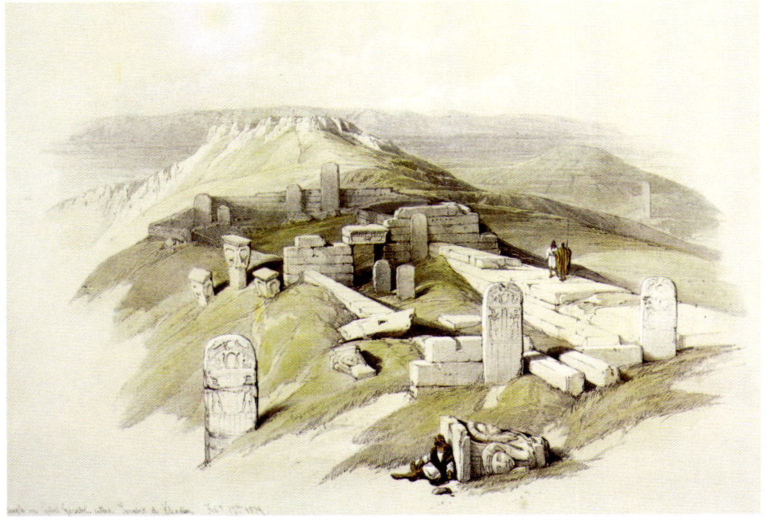

An Ancient Egyptian Temple on Gebel Garabe

And when all the land of Egypt was famished, the people cried to Pharaoh for bread: and Pharaoh said unto all the Egyptians, Go unto Joseph; what he saith to you, do (Gen. 41:55).

"What could have been the intent of these temples and memorial stones in the midst of solitude and silence, in this lone and distant land with which they would seem to have no possible connection? This is a point wrapped in the darkness of time, and which the hand of modern science has not yet unveiled."

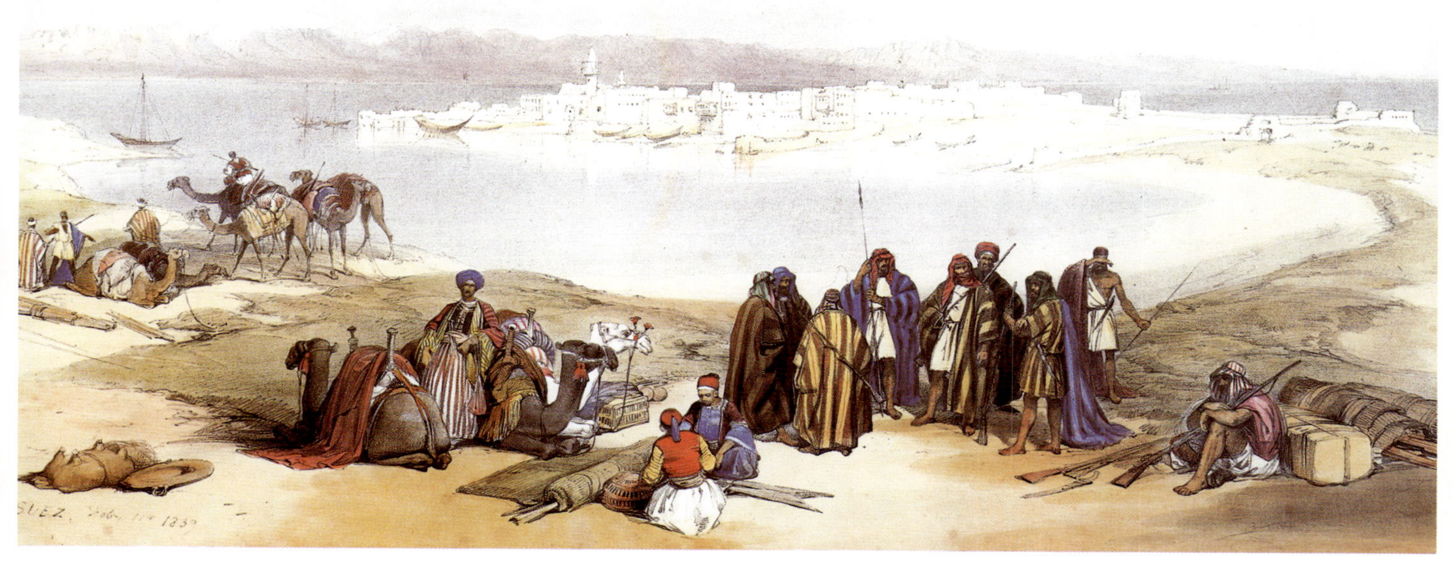

General View of Suez

And Moses stretched out his hand over the sea; and the Lord caused the sea to go [back] by a strong east wind all that night, and made the sea dry [land], and the waters were divided (Exod. 14:21).

The place of the passage of the Israelites has excited much learned inquiry. The more probable conception is that the passage was made across the small arm of the sea which runs up by Suez, a breadth of less than four miles. From the Sacred Narrative, a north wind blew "all night," uncovering the shoals above the site of Suez, and in the "morning watch" the sea returned. Thus, not more than two or three hours seem to have been allotted for the passage of three million of people. The miracle consisted not in the march of the people but in the divine direction of the wind; and the return of the waters at the command of Moses.

Side View of the Great Sphinx

Then Pharaoh called for Moses and Aaron in haste; and he said, I have sinned against the Lord your God, and against you (Exod. 10:16).

The mutilated state of this enormous figure is perhaps more strikingly observed in profile than in front . . . undisturbed possession of its solitude is left to the Great Sphinx, the most extraordinary of the productions of man in this land of his wonders. After drawing and studying it, Mr. Roberts said that he had more powerful emotions excited by it than by the Pyramids. That the Sphinx was worshipped, there is no doubt;

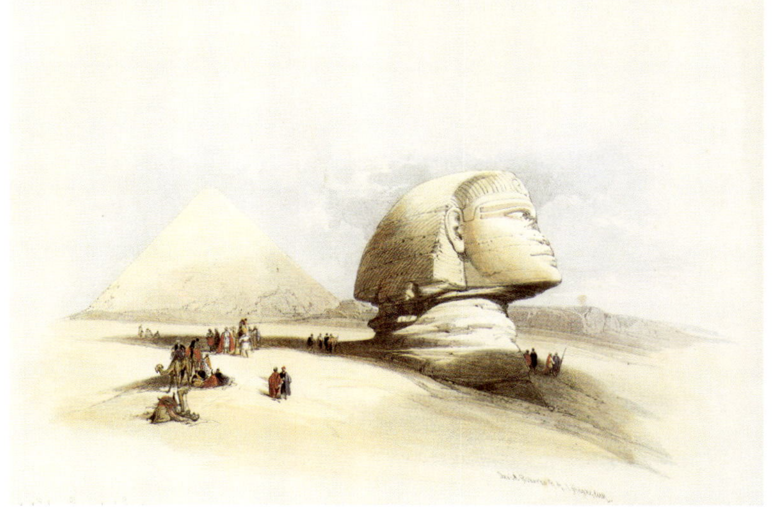

Pyramids of Geezeh (Gizah) from the Nile

Thus saith the Lord, In this thou shalt know that I [am] the Lord: behold, I will smite with the rod that [is] in mine hand upon the waters which [are] in the river, and they shall be turned to blood (Exod. 7:17).

When the river is low and the intersecting canals dry and practicable, the journey from Grand Cairo to the pyramids of Geezeh is a ride of little more than an hour. The traveller mounts in the streets of New Cairo and rides to Old Cairo, where he crosses the Nile at the Madiah, or ferry, to a village the nearest to the pyramids, though five miles distant from them, called Geezeh, whence the association of its name with these wonders of Egypt and the world. From across the Nile the appearance of these stupendous constructions is that which is here represented.

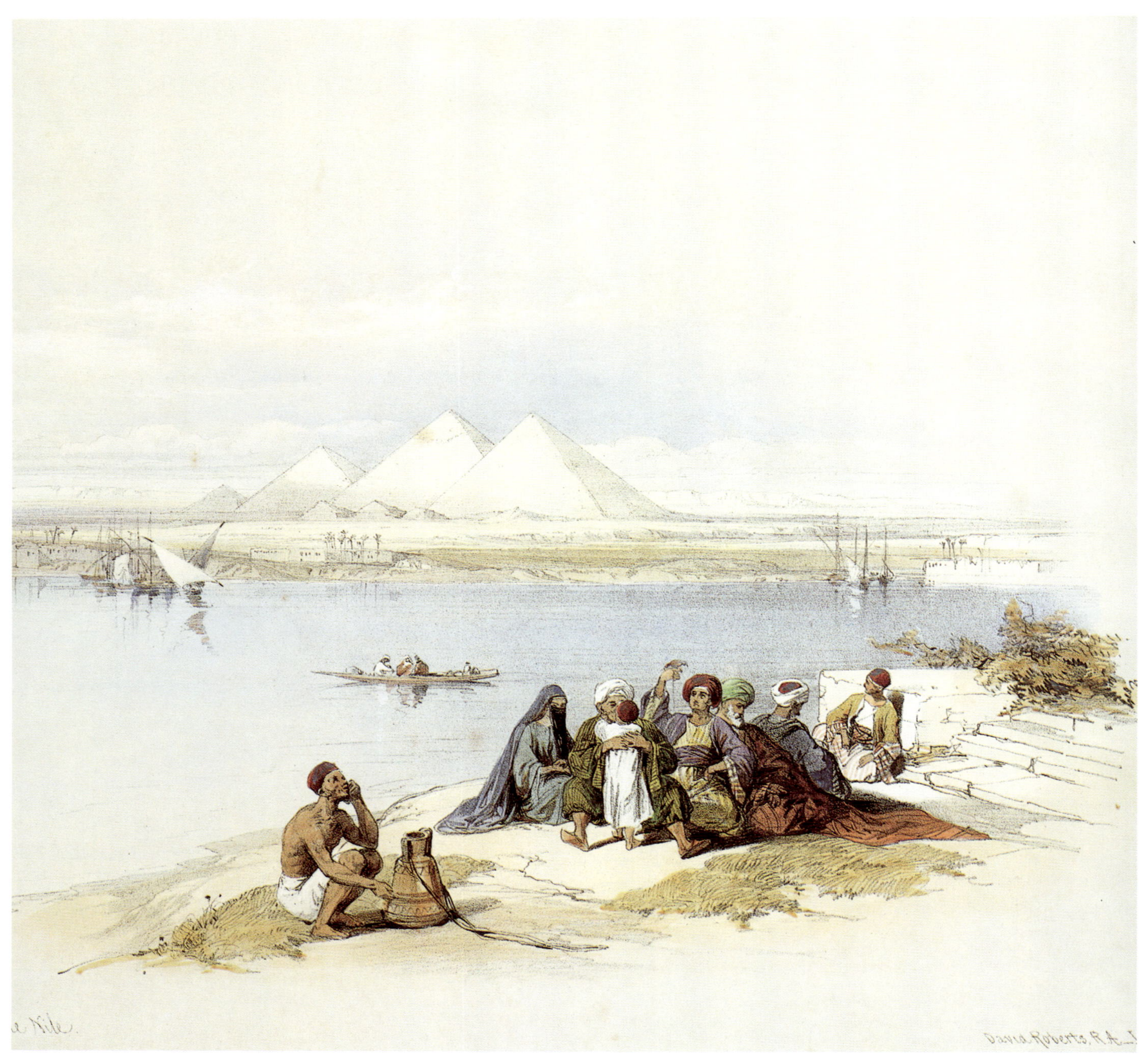

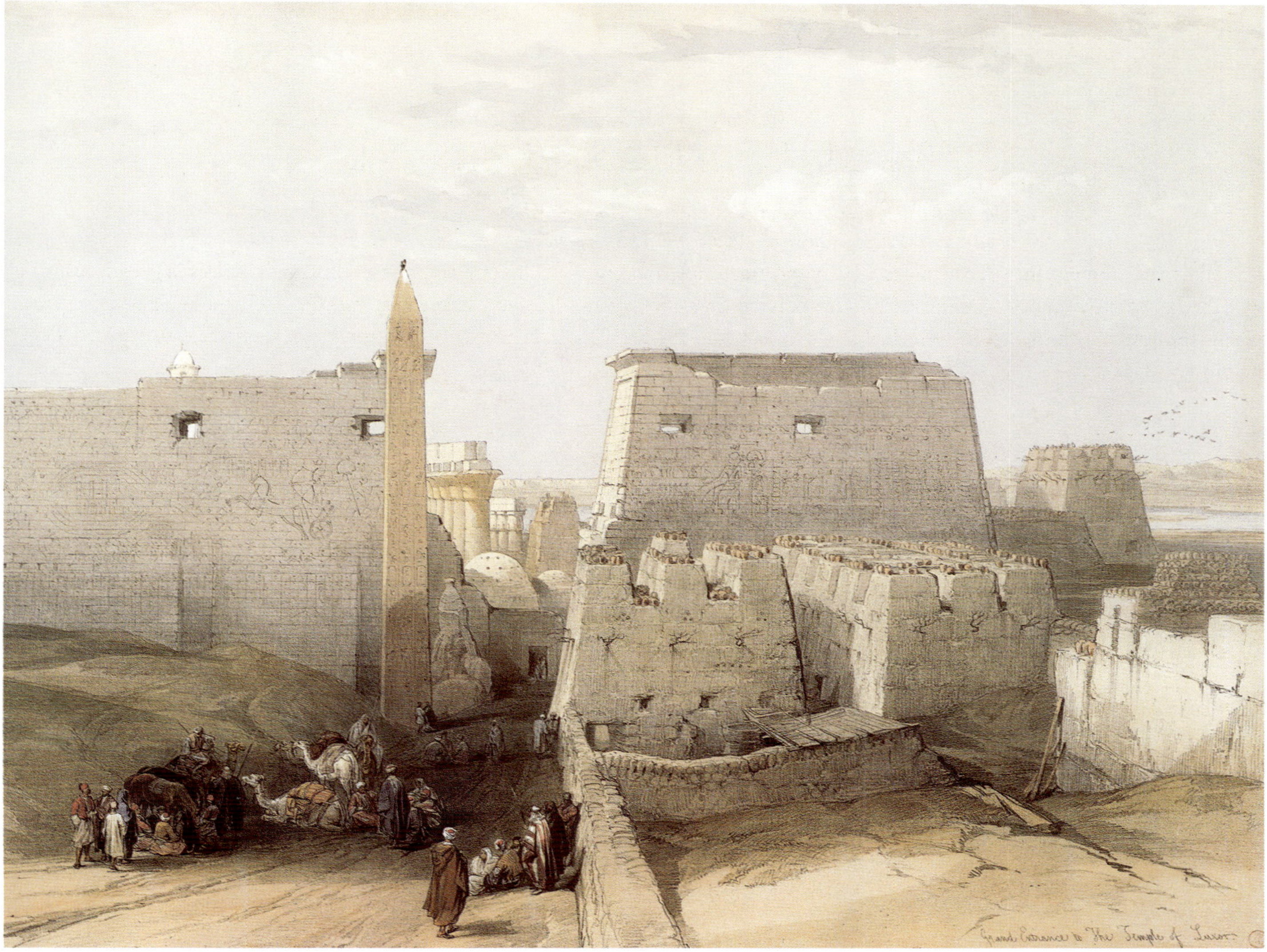

Grand Entrance to the Temple of Luxor

I will lay thy cities waste, and thou shalt be desolate,
and thou shalt know that I [am] the LORD (Ezek. 35:4).

"How beautiful, how grand the approach to Luxor must have been ..." This sketch is made from the summit of a mount that overlooks the huts of the village of Luxor . . . it is here that the vast propylon and the remaining Obelisk . . . are best seen. . . . The propyla are enriched with elaborate sculpture, recording the military deeds and conquests of Ramesses II.

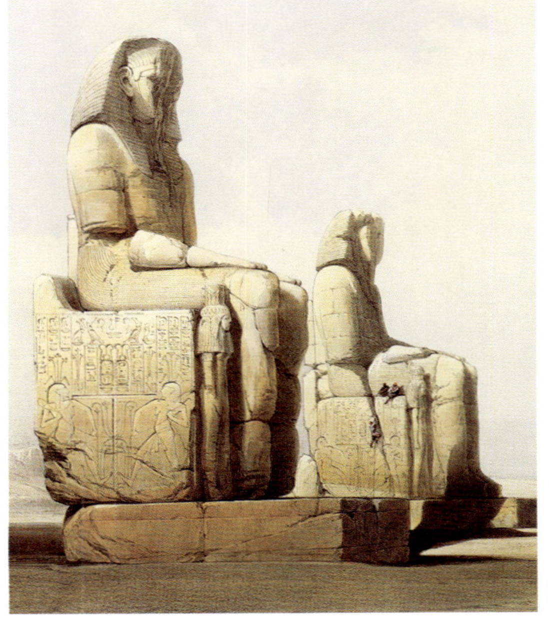

Thebes, the Colossal Statues of Amunoph III

And I will pour my fury upon Sin, the strength of Egypt; and I will cut off the multitude of No. And I will set fire in Egypt: Sin shall have great pain, and No shall be rent asunder, and Noph [shall have] distresses daily (Ezek. 30:15-16).

These enormous figures rest where they did at the period of their erection, when they formed the entrance of a grand dromos to the temple, 1100 feet in length. A line of hieroglyphics extends from the shoulder down the back to the pedestal, and here is found the name of the pharaoh whom the statue represented, Amunoph III.

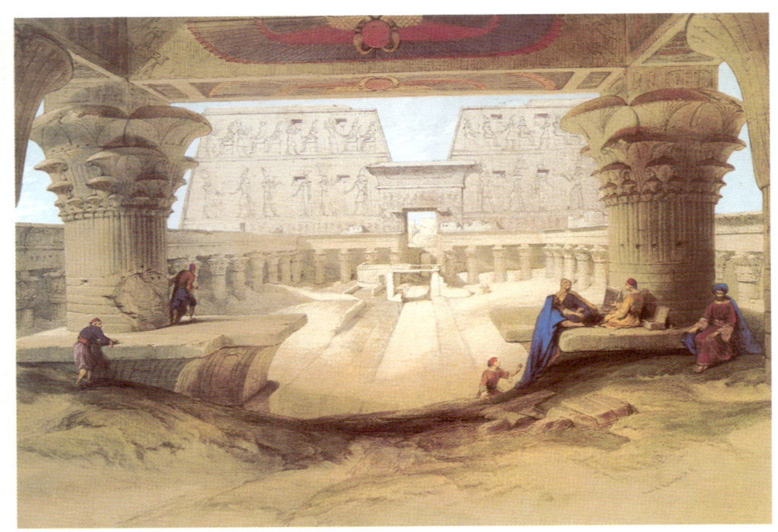

View from the Portico of the Temple of Edfou (Edfu), Upper Egypt

For I will pass through the land of Egypt this night, and will smite all the firstborn in the land of Egypt, both man and beast; and against all the gods of Egypt I will execute judgment: I [am] the Lord (Exod. 12:12).

This view . . . looking across the peristyle court of the temple . . . is one of striking magnificence. The cloistered corridor, covered with painted hieroglyphics, offered its shelter from an Egyptian sun to the priests and those permitted to enter the sacred precincts. The vast faces of the towers are covered with gigantic figures . . . and represent the offerings made by the pharaohs to the gods.

Front Elevation of the Great Temple of Aboo-Simbel (Abu-Simbel)

And the kings of the earth, and the great men . . . and the mighty men . . . hid themselves in the dens and in the rocks of the mountains (Rev. 6:15).
Here, at the Temple of Osiris, four colossal giants . . . are seated on thrones. These awful idols seemed to sit there waiting for some great summons which should awaken and reanimate these *"Kings of the earth who lie in glory, every one in his own house."*

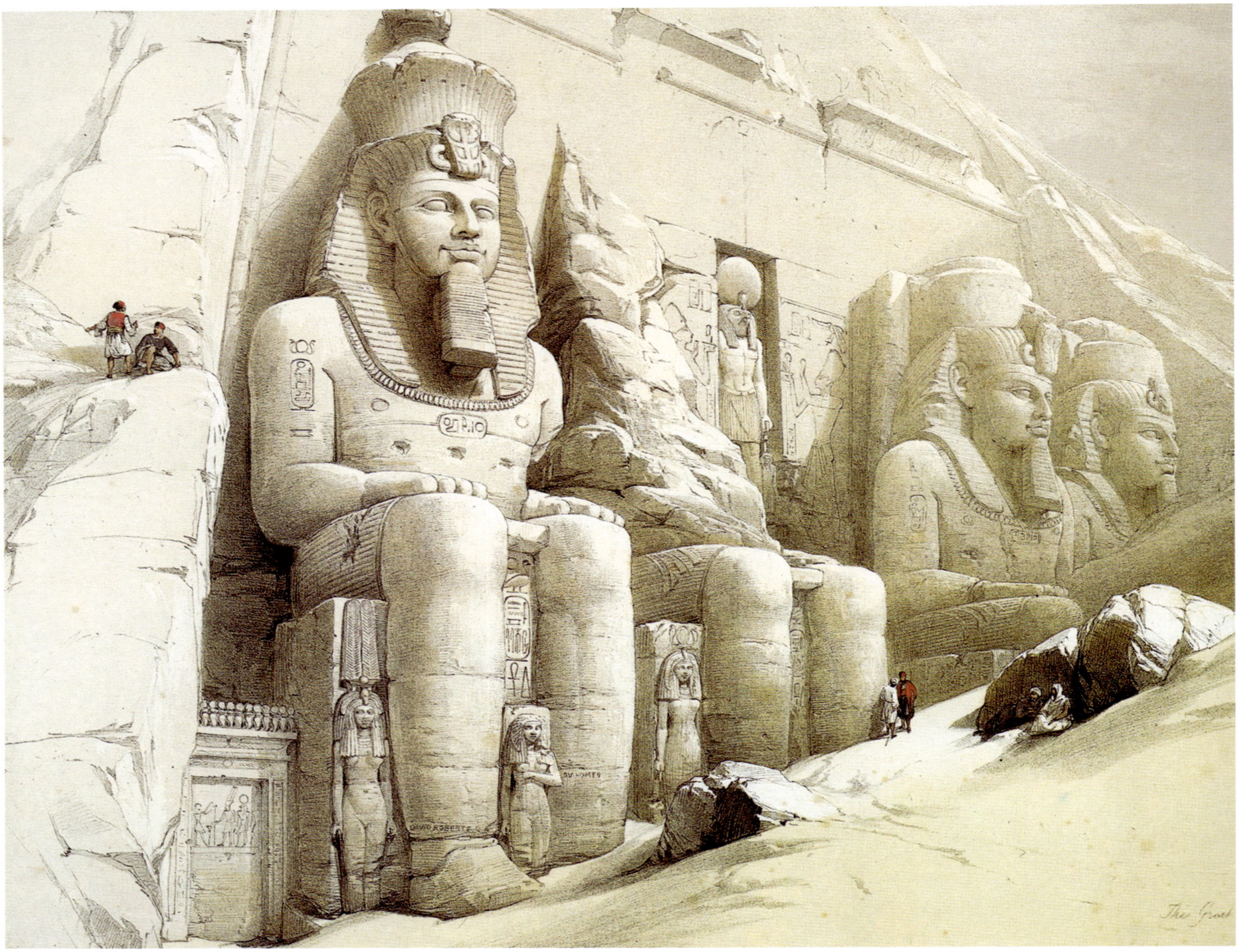